The Clash of
Tongues
with Glimpses of Revival

Other books by the same author:

Reflections on the Baptism in the Holy Spirit
Reflections on the Gifts of the Spirit
Reflections on a Song of Love (1 Cor 13)
A Trumpet Call to Women
Consider Him
Battle for the Body

In course of preparation:

The Incomparable Christ
Christian Fundamentals
Pioneers of the Spiritual Way
Reflections on Abraham
Reflections on Moses

The Clash of Tongues
with Glimpses of Revival

Hugh B. Black

NEW DAWN BOOKS
GREENOCK, SCOTLAND

© Hugh B. Black 1988

First published 1988 by
NEW DAWN BOOKS
27 Denholm Street, Greenock PA16 8RH, Scotland.

ISBN 1 870944 06 2

Unless otherwise stated biblical quotations are from the
Revised Version

Cover photo: Craig Richardson

Production and printing in England for
NEW DAWN BOOKS
27 Denholm Street, Greenock PA16 8RH, Scotland
by Nuprint Ltd, Harpenden, Herts AL5 4SE.

Dedication

To the memory of George Jeffreys who did so much to pioneer Pentecostal truths in Britain. I benefited greatly from his life and work.

Acknowledgements

I am grateful to all those who continue to encourage me to write; to my daughter Dr Alison H. Black for editing the manuscript and transcribing the basic text of Part 2 from tape recordings; to my wife Isobel and to Miss Pauline Anderson, Mr Alistair Duff and Miss Jennifer Jack for proof-reading and helpful advice; and to my daughter Mrs Grace Gault for assistance with Greek references. In addition, I am indebted to Miss Anderson for visiting Lewis and going over the draft of Mrs Mary MacLean's testimony with her. My thanks are again due to Miss Irene Morrison for her generous help in typing a great part of the manuscript.

Again I must acknowledge Dr Gordon D. Fee's *The First Epistle to the Corinthians*. I am also indebted to Dr Donald Lee Barnett and Jeffrey P. McGregor for their *Speaking in Other Tongues*—particularly for the evidence they produce for Finney, Moody and Spurgeon having spoken in tongues. I have pleasure in recommending both of these scholarly works. My thanks are due to other authors and publishers from whose works various extracts have been taken.

Contents

PART 2: GLIMPSES OF REVIVAL
   (With the Testimony of Mary MacLean)

APPENDICES

Foreword

When my father asked me to write a Foreword to this book I do not know whether he remembered that my acquaintance with the manuscript has almost as long a history as his own. It was as a child, sitting in the morning meetings of a Church Camp in Perthshire, that I first listened to his exposition of a part of 1 Corinthians 14. This was a Camp at which a breath of revival stirred, immediately after my father's return from one of his later visits to the Island of Lewis. One might say that I grew up on stories of the Lewis revival and Pentecostal exegesis; unlike some temperaments, mine was one that thrived on both. Since the charismatic movement had not yet risen to endow Pentecostalism with a measure of respectability in the eyes of the rest of the world, there was an added element of zest in the debate that moulded the exegesis.

If the exposition of the scriptural basis of Pentecostal practices brought a satisfaction that was partly intellectual, the appeal of stories about revival (including my father's own experiences in Lewis) was, I believe, wholly spiritual. It is one thing to hear or read sensational reports of visions, community-wide repentance, dramatic conversions, and other outstanding miracles. It is quite another thing to sense the atmosphere of that other world that is so close to us, but not so clearly perceived by most, as it comes to be in times of revival. The draw that comes on the soul is the draw of God Himself, and of His Christ. Some fear that encounter and flee precipitately from it; if they only knew, 'Thou dravest Love from thee, who dravest Me.' The fire burns, but only those who shun it need dread its burning; it is the revealer of Christ.

Readers of Part 2 of this book will be struck by the quality of revival fire that burned in Mary MacLean, a daughter of Lewis. Not a sensation-seeker nor a limelight seeker (she shied away from even ordinary forms of social entertainment), she enjoyed a deep and sweet relationship with Christ and knew also the burden of a Church and of a world in a way that brought its own measure of the 'sensational.' But for her, 'revival' was not only a community-wide phenomenon; it was not too profound a term to describe the individual soul's awakening to Christ. To the record of her life conveyed in these pages I would add my own impression on meeting her, of an eminently sane and level-headed, gentle but clear-sighted person.

I recommend the reader's attention particularly to the opening chapters of Part 2. The relation between Pentecost and revival is a timely subject not often (if ever) dealt with so directly and concretely. Part 1 opens Pentecost to the evangelical's intellect; Part 2 opens it to his spirit by showing it in a revival setting. May the controversy aroused by the 'clash of tongues' not distract any seeker from his spiritual birthright.

Alison H. Black

Preface

The publication of *The Clash of Tongues: with Glimpses of Revival* has posed a problem. It is one in a series of five books, the other four being *Reflections on the Baptism of the Holy Spirit*, *Reflections on the Gifts of the Spirit*, *Reflections on a Song of Love (1 Cor 13)* and *A Trumpet Call to Women*. The other books were written in 1987/88 whereas much of the present one was written almost forty years earlier but left unpublished. A certain amount of the material produced then has been used in the other works and the question arises as to whether this study should merely be brought up to date and left with most of its original material retained or whether parts incorporated in the other studies should now be omitted. It has been decided to follow the first course since many readers may not, in fact, go through all five books systematically. It is recognised that there will be a measure of overlap for those who do.

The preface written in 1947 is perhaps the most dated part of the early manuscript but it occurred to me that readers might be interested to see this and compare the position as it appeared to me then with the present position. I wrote:

There are perhaps few chapters in the New Testament which are less understood than 1 Corinthians 14. Some have regarded it as unimportant—holding the view that there Paul was mainly giving instruction on spiritual gifts. These, they thought, were associated with 'a primitive and transitory' phase in Christian experience. Hence they feel the chapter is outdated—although both the subject with which Paul dealt, and the instructions given, were more or less beyond their comprehension. Widely varied and generally inconsistent views to explain the phenomena have been advanced by this school and in many cases the subject has been dismissed as altogether inconsequential.

There is a second identifiable group of a strongly fundamentalist outlook which tends to find the chapter almost embarrassing. There is much in it which emerges too clearly to be denied—but the acceptance of it cuts across established views and practices. The result of this is sometimes an unacceptable misinterpretation of the text. This school generally takes the view that the gifts were for the beginning of the Christian dispensation and that tongues, interpretation and prophecy have passed away.

To a third group largely comprising the Pentecostal churches the chapter has long been precious and of fundamental importance. But even here a great deal of misunderstanding exists. This arises from two main sources:

1. The matter dealt with is complex and at least superficially seems to contain irreconcilable difficulties.

2. The first difficulty is intensified because of a general lack of spiritual depth and insight in our day. This did not arise to anything like the same extent in the 'mystic' East of Paul's day, and it is primarily with deep spiritual matters that the chapter deals. These never were, nor ever could be, naturally discerned. The natural man, as Paul wrote elsewhere, cannot discern the things of the Spirit for spiritual things are spiritually discerned.

It is hoped that this book will have something for all three groups. There are already signs that the first group is changing in its attitude to spiritual gifts; healing is now increasingly widely sought and practised. Psychology and philosophy are increasingly revealing that there are parts in human personality the existence of which was undreamed of until fairly recent times. Instead of the gifts of the Spirit being associated with the 'primitive and rudimentary' it may very well be that they will become more generally associated with the 'illumined and mature.' Certainly many of the older philosophies, which gave reason an undue place, are now discredited (see Appendix 1). Mind alone, as never before, is seen to be at the 'end of its tether.' The fundamental problems of philosophy are no nearer solution by this means than when first examined. Many of the deepest thinkers are increasingly turning to religion for an answer and explanation of life. The latest developments in certain of the sciences, such as astronomy and physics, have tended to support a religious interpretation of the universe. To turn to religion is no form of escapism. Philosophy always has recognised the possibility of reaching the ultimates in a mystic way. There is nothing irrational in this, and it is exactly what Christianity does. The approach is supra-rational;[1] but in so being is not irrational, and when a person goes this way no violence is done to the intellect. Rather is reason transcended and in being transcended is used at its highest. Things more fundamental than mind are emerging in man and the stage is rapidly being set for the sincere and intellectual inquirer to adopt a new attitude to spiritual gifts and the miraculous in religion. There is not, nor has there ever been, any real clash between true science and true religion—nor is there between modern psychology and religion. Indeed, properly understood, these last go hand in hand. Truth is ever welcome to the sincere, and it can be said with confidence that the ablest and best, intellectually and morally, will find illumination and blessing in a return to the early practices of the Church.

The attitude of the second group to the miraculous gifts is also tending to change. The tremendous impact which Pentecost has made on both the Church and the world cannot be ignored. The power and growth of the Movement are phenomenal, and many sincere fundamentalists have recognised these things. A movement which is so faithful to Scripture and whose phenomenal growth, liberality and missionary zeal are demonstrated on all sides, is increasingly demanding respect. In the Scandinavian countries and America particularly, it holds an honoured place and many now feel that it is indeed what it has long claimed to be—a movement enjoying the promised outpouring of the Holy Spirit in the last days. Much of the earlier opposition has died and a more interested and inquiring attitude has taken its place. It is hoped that this school also may derive benefit from the ensuing pages.

The third group the writer has borne continually in mind. This group is more familiar with the subject matter and will find that the difficult problems have not been glossed over. Rather have these been sought and honestly faced. Some of the more prominent may be instanced:

1. How can an individual be edified through speaking something which he cannot understand?

2. What is the point of speaking in this way when the hearers do not understand either?

3. Is there a spiritual means of communication between the human spirit and God which by-passes the intellect and yields benefit?

4. If the gifts are gifts of the Spirit, how can error creep into their use?

5. Do the regulations which Paul lays down clash with the direct unctioning of the Spirit upon an individual? and if not, why, for example, does he require to say that no one

is to give a public utterance in tongues if there is no interpreter present in the church, since tongues are a gift of the Spirit? Surely such a person would not be unctioned in any case if it was wrong for him to give forth! Are there in fact two conflicting authorities: Paul's writing and the direct voice of the Spirit?

6. If tongues are a sign to the unbeliever, and prophecy to the believer, how do we reconcile the words 'If . . . all speak with tongues, and there come in men unlearned or unbelieving, will they not say that ye are mad? But if all prophesy . . . [they will declare] that God is among you indeed'? To whom was the 'sign'—believer or unbeliever? Have the translators or the early copyists erred or is the matter quite understandable?

7. How many may prophesy in one service? One verse says: 'let the prophets prophesy by two or three'; another says, 'ye may all prophesy, one by one.' Which is it? The corollary of the explanation of this is most interesting, and if correct, is of particular significance, affecting the number of utterances in tongues permissible in one service.

8. Tongues, according to verse 2 and other references, are Godward. How then is interpretation in modern times so often manward? Surely if God is addressed in one, He will be addressed in the other. Is there Scriptural justification for the present-day practice?

9. Was there a difference between the tongues of Acts 2, which were understood by foreigners, and the 'tongues' of 1 Corinthians 14 which 'no man' understood?

10. Was the meeting in the Upper Room different in kind, or conduct, from the type of church meeting for which Paul legislates in 1 Corinthians 14? Would the first have conformed to those regulations—for example, in number of utterances in tongues, and in the interpretation and orderly course of these?

These and other points are dealt with as they arise in the text, and it is hoped that both spiritual and intellectual *benefit may be derived from the perusal of the solutions offered.*

The years have brought a tremendous change. Many who at one time would have been numbered in the first category identified are now in the Charismatic movement, and this movement has had a world-wide impact.

The second grouping has also been radically affected. Many who were once opposed to Pentecost have been moved of God. Much of the old opposition has died and indeed this group has supplied many of today's leaders.

The third group has continued to grow world-wide. While emphases of doctrine differ between 'Charismatics' and 'Pentecostals' and indeed between sub-groupings of both, the fact is that there has been, and there continues to be, a tremendous outpouring of the Holy Spirit upon the Church. The expectations voiced in 1947 are being wonderfully fulfilled and I believe 'the best is yet to be.'

Now although there may be much more light on Pentecostal truths in 1987 than there was in 1947, there remains a good deal of difficulty for many in understanding 1 Corinthians 14, and of course the problems referred to in the earlier preface remain.

Part 1 of this book is not confined to a narrow academic interpretation of 1 Corinthians 14. Indeed it may appear to the reader that the chapter has almost been used as a launching pad from which I have gone out to the consideration of themes like the Baptism in the Holy Spirit, the gifts of tongues, interpretation and prophecy and various spiritual principles as they have risen in the text. This particular portion of Scripture was initially chosen (forty years ago) since it seemed a good place from which to explore the whole field of Pentecostal doctrine which, in that earlier day, was much misunderstood.

One result of this type of approach is an unusual number of appendices but it is hoped that both they and the main text will prove helpful to readers.[2]

As I have explained in an earlier book, readers have suggested that I should include testimonies in my writings. I have followed the advice and generally look for stories which will be particularly appropriate to the works published. For Part 2 of this book I have chosen the testimony of an old Highland lady who was deeply involved in the 1939 revival in Lewis and later in the revival associated with the late Rev Duncan Campbell.

Her story is of unusual interest. In addition to a rare depth of spiritual insight, Mrs MacLean has experienced a series of quite remarkable visions which have been accurately fulfilled. She has been a veritable seer.

Coming from a traditional Christian background this lady had not been instructed in Pentecostal doctrine, but in 1939 when the Spirit of God was moving deeply she found herself speaking in tongues, of which she had had no earlier knowledge. When I met her over thirty years ago this happened to her again and there came understanding of the Scriptural nature of her experience. The gift has never left her.

Her testimony seems to me to be particularly appropriate in a work which amongst other things seeks to identify the link between Pentecost and historic revival.

Note

[1] C.E.M. Joad indicated that very possibly the next advance in human knowledge would be precisely in this realm.

[2] *After completing the text of Part 1, I became acquainted with the work of Dr Gordon D. Fee:* The First Epistle to the Corinthians *(in* The New International Commentary on the New Testament *series, ed. F. F. Bruce (Wm. B. Eerdmans Publishing Company, 1987). This has had an influence on my view of the limitation of utterances in tongues and prophecy in one service. Accordingly, I advise readers to consult the italicised note on pp.96–97 before reading and becoming unnecessarily involved in the text of chap. 13.*

PART 1:

THE CLASH OF TONGUES
(A Commentary on 1 Corinthians 14)

1

General Introduction

1 Corinthians 14 deals with the regulation of certain gifts of the Spirit, and these are difficult to understand if the experience with which they are frequently associated is not itself first understood. This experience is widely known as the Baptism in the Spirit—predicted by John the Baptist, promised by Christ, and first experienced on the day of Pentecost.

John said: '. . . he that cometh after me is mightier than I, whose shoes I am not worthy to bear: he shall baptize you with the Holy Ghost and with fire' (Mt 3:11). Thus Christ was referred to as the Baptizer in the Holy Spirit.

Towards the close of His ministry, He Himself spoke much of the Holy Spirit. Earlier He had spoken of the 'living water': 'He that believeth on me, as the scripture hath said, out of his belly shall flow rivers of living water. But this spake he of the Spirit, which they that believed on him were to receive' (Jn 7:38–39). But as His days drew to a close, He began to give more particular instruction and teaching regarding the Holy Spirit. He told His disciples that He was glad for their sakes that He was leaving them, for otherwise the Comforter, the Spirit of Truth, could not come; and He, when He was come, would guide them into all truth. He would take of the things of Christ and reveal them to them. He would convict of sin, righteousness and judgment.

As the time of His final departure from earth drew nearer, His preaching became still more personal and particular. After the resurrection He breathed on them and said: 'Receive ye the Holy Spirit.' This was not fulfilled at that time. It was really a commandment or injunction carrying with it a promise of fulfilment. 'The Spirit,' He had said, 'abideth *with* you, and shall be *in* you' (Jn 14:17). Undoubtedly they were born of the Spirit. He, the Spirit, was with them—but something different and distinctive was still to happen. He was to enter *in* and possess them. The accompanying power of God was no longer to exercise remote control, as it were, from without. He was to become their possessing power.

'Go,' said Christ, 'into all the world and preach the gospel, making disciples,' but He also said, 'tarry ye in the city of Jerusalem, until ye be endued with power from on high (Lk 24:49 AV); and again, 'ye shall receive power, when the Holy Ghost is come upon you: and ye shall be my witnesses, both in Jerusalem and in Judea and in Samaria and unto the uttermost parts of the earth' (Acts 1:8).

These men who had known Christ personally so long, who had been in His inner circle, who had heard His deepest teaching, and who had witnessed His greatest miracles, were evidently considered quite unable to fulfil their great mission without their Baptism in the Spirit. They were still to be radically affected. The witnessing of the crucifixion was not destined to make the change, nor was the glory and power of the resurrection. One thing, and one alone, was essential: the enduement of power from on high—the experience of the day of Pentecost. '*When* (*After*:AV) the Holy Spirit is come upon you,' said Christ, 'ye shall receive power.'

Peter, who trembled and cursed before a servant maid, is to be transformed in a few short days. Fearlessly he is to accuse the assembled thousands in Jerusalem of the murder of Christ, and instead of being torn to pieces by the fanatical mob who had so lately committed that murder, he is to see fear fall upon them; they are to be 'pricked to the heart' and cry out for salvation. What has to happen in the interim? Peter is to be baptized in the Spirit, and in being baptized is to be transformed.

It is difficult to over-emphasise the importance of this Baptism, or the place which Christ gave to the ministry of the Spirit. The whole record of the progress of the Church of Christ is a record of the work of the Spirit. It *is* His work. Now the question arises: if these apostles who were so deeply privileged in knowing Christ personally had such a deep need—where do Christians stand today? Two further questions emerge: (1) Has the Church generally received this experience? (2) If she has not, how may she receive it?

In Acts 2 the Spirit was initially outpoured. In that chapter, which is dealt with more fully later, the record of the Baptism of the hundred and twenty is given. They were all together in one place tarrying for the promised outpouring. Suddenly from Heaven there came the sound of a mighty rushing wind which filled the place; they were all filled with the Holy Spirit. Upon each of them abode a cloven tongue like as of fire and all spoke in tongues as the Spirit gave them utterance.

On five occasions including the day of Pentecost, record is given of individuals being baptized in the Holy Spirit. In three groups—the company at Pentecost, the Ephesian twelve, Cornelius and his household—it is recorded that those baptized spoke in tongues. In Paul's case we are not told what happened at his Baptism but later we read that he spoke in tongues more than all the Corinthians and in the final case—that of the Samaritans—we read that Simon

Magus coveted the ability to lay on hands because he *saw* that through this the Holy Spirit was given. Thus, outward manifestation of the inner experience was always evident.

That such phenomena did not cease on the day of Pentecost, nor were peculiar to the early days of the Church alone, is evident from the case of the Ephesian twelve of Acts 19. After their baptism in water these men had Paul's hands laid on them and were baptized in the Spirit, speaking with tongues. Whether they were Christians or not when Paul met them may be doubtful, but that they were Christians before they were baptized in water is certain, for in the New Testament none were baptized *before* they believed. In what way, then, was their position different, after baptism in water and before Paul's hands came upon them, from the position of tens of thousands of Christians today, who have been saved and baptized in water but have not been taken on to the next stage as the Ephesian twelve were? Many stop short at this point and mistakenly think that they are filled with the Spirit. Surely their position is identical with that of the group whom Paul met and baptized, before the point where he laid hands on them. How long, then, are such experiences with their accompanying supernatural phenomena to continue? 'The promise,' said Peter (of the outpouring of the Spirit), 'is to you (i.e. to the Jews in Jerusalem to whom he preached) and to your children (i.e. to the generation following) and to as many as are afar off.' How many? 'Even as many as the Lord our God shall call.' That surely takes us to the end of the dispensation and to the completion of the Church—a time still future. History, of course, gives considerable evidence of the continuance of these experiences and of the exercise of spiritual gifts through the centuries between Peter's day and our own. Neither in Scripture nor in history is there evidence for the view that these were for a transition period, and were soon to cease.

How then is the experience to be obtained? The

command was, 'Tarry *until* ye be endued with power from on high.' The injunction still stands. The experience is to be deeply sought by prayer and sincere waiting before God in a clean condition.[1] No man can give himself, or his fellow, the experience. It comes down from above. God is still sovereign and in this realm man must take his proper suppliant place. There is nothing to do but be in God's will and, in expectant faith, wait. God does it. In His own time and way His Power comes. The seeker must then be careful to obey the Spirit. If this is done, an experience similar to that of the disciples on the day of Pentecost can be expected. In Scripture there were two ways in which the experience was received: first spontaneously from Heaven as on the day of Pentecost and in the case of Cornelius—and secondly through the laying on of hands as in the other three recorded cases.

Now it is against the background of this experience that we go on to study the operation and regulation of the gifts of the Spirit in 1 Corinthians 14—tongues, interpretation and prophecy in particular.[2]

Notes

[1] This is important. He came down on a prepared company at Pentecost. When the dove which Noah sent out of the ark found nothing but carrion flesh it returned to him, nor would it settle until a clean resting place was found. The Spirit never settles on that which is unclean.

[2] Is it possible for an individual to exercise a gift of the Spirit without having been baptized in the Spirit? From Scripture there seems to be no positive evidence that such happened in New Testament days. It is difficult, however, to deny that some do exercise genuine gifts, for example healing and faith, without having first experienced Baptism similar to that of the early disciples. Undoubtedly men are often mightily unctioned by God, even if they have not been fully baptized—and it may be possible to exercise certain of the gifts without this full experience.

2

The Corinthian Background

In an earlier book in this series (*Reflections on the Gifts of the Spirit*), I wrote a postscript on the Corinth of Paul's day and sketched the situation that faced him in the church there. This is so pertinent for the present study that I am incorporating most of it in this chapter.

Previously a Greek city state, Corinth had been destroyed and a century later refounded as a Roman colony by Julius Caesar. It was very prosperous and became notorious for vice. To 'act like a Corinthian'[1] was another way of saying 'to commit fornication.' Sexual vice was particularly rampant, as indeed it was in 'any seaport where money was plentiful and prostitutes of both sexes readily available. The population was cosmopolitan, including amongst others Romans, Greeks and Jews. The major part were descended from freed Roman slaves. Paul's Corinth has been described as the New York, Los Angeles and Las Vegas of the ancient world.'[2] The young church reflected the society from which its members came. Mainly gentiles, formerly idolators, they had been in the habit of going to temple feasts and immorality had been for many a way of life. There were wide divisions in the church, not only of race—Roman, Greek, Jew—but between freedman and slaves and between rich and poor. Hellenistic influences were strong and Fee could write, 'Although they were the Christian church in Corinth, an inordinate amount of Corinth was yet in them.'[3] Paul had founded the church and, while at Ephesus two years later, had sent them a letter which dealt with problems of immorality and idolatry. They had resented this and had written to him. His reply to this is our First Epistle to the Corinthians. It is the third point of contact Paul had with this church. Tension had risen between Paul and them. He wrote to regulate eleven specific matters—ten of which were behavioural. The influence of Roman and Hellenic thought was very great and many of the abuses with which Paul had to deal arose from those influences. It would seem that with a degree of arrogance many in the church regarded themselves as deeply spiritual. They tended to despise the body, considering that they had reached a plane above body. This led in two opposite directions— one to a permissive attitude to immorality and the other to an asceticism which despised normal marriage relation- ships. There is some evidence that they regarded speaking in tongues as a mark of super-spirituality. They seem to have believed that they were sharing the language of angels and to have assumed that they were thereby already enjoy- ing a heavenly life—this in spite of the gross immorality that was in their midst, about which they were seemingly quite unperturbed. Paul had to bring them down to earth. He dealt with true spirituality and morality, and the proper functioning of the gifts of the Spirit, including tongues. The Corinthians were also particularly interested in knowledge and wisdom and he had to regulate their thinking on this as well, not only in relation to the gifts but in more general terms. While there were divisions amongst them which Paul cited as an evidence of their carnality (shown in their lawsuits with each other), the main thrust of his letter does not deal so much with divisions between factions within the church as with matters that lay between Paul and the church—e.g. heresies that had risen and were taking them in a Hellenic direction away from both Paul and the gospel he preached. He sought to bring them back to a right foundation and to encourage a proper attitude to his own apostleship which they were evidently questioning. They seem to have had some doubt about this and the degree of his spirituality. They learned! In no apologetic mood Paul goes into battle. His sword is sharp and his teachings have echoed down the years influencing the lives of untold millions. An understanding of the background of this epistle brings home something of the awful pain Paul experienced when his children in Christ turned aside. I have personally sensed this recently as never before. I can in a measure understand what he meant in another context: 'My little children, of whom I am again in travail until Christ be formed in you' (Gal 4:19). Paul was up against strong opposition—but in the end he conquered.

Notes
[1] Fee, *First Epistle to the Corinthians*, p.2.
[2] *Ibid.*, p.3.
[3] *Ibid.*, p.4.

3

Introduction to 1 Corinthians 14

The Corinthians were greatly taken up with tongues, which they believed were angelic, and the main purpose of 1 Corinthians 14 is to regulate the use of the vocal gifts of the Spirit, and in particular to discourage the wrong use of the gift of tongues. This last may be summed up in one sentence: Tongues without interpretation are out of order and are not to be permitted. Obviously it was common for the Corinthians to have more than one person speaking in tongues at the same time in their public worship, and for these utterances to go uninterpreted. Paul writes against this and also shows the superior merits of the less spectacular gift of prophecy.[1] Almost the whole chapter hinges upon those two points.

Now Paul's teaching on tongues here immediately raises one of the problems of Acts 2, since on that occasion all spoke in tongues and probably all spoke at the same time and without intepretation. This is forbidden now, so there must obviously be a difference between conduct in the initial Baptism and normal church procedure. How can this be explained? In Acts 2 the people were waiting to receive the fulfilment of the promise of the outpouring of the Holy Spirit—the main emphasis was on receiving from God. In 1 Corinthians 14 the church is viewed as gathered together for worship and there would be an emphasis on giving to God. Now at the time of the Baptism in the Spirit people are being initiated into a new spiritual realm. Christ's saying is being fulfilled. The true worshippers are worshipping in spirit and in truth. Power comes mightily upon them and often they are unsure how to conduct themselves. There are sometimes manifestations which are caused by the unyieldingness of the flesh, and this can perplex onlookers, but when there is complete obedience to the Spirit, Baptisms are most beautiful to witness. Anything distasteful is attributable to man—God being ever the author of perfection. There may of course be, and generally there is, a deep awe accompanying these experiences which in itself causes a certain shrinking in natural man, but that is as it should be.

But when we come to the public assembly, the vessels empowered and filled earlier are expected to conduct themselves differently.[2] No longer are they in the initial stage of the experience but should be developing into controlled and seasoned vessels. In the forming of the channels, as it were, at the Baptism, they may have acted in ways which are not always to be repeated. Some of the physical manifestations may have resulted from resistance to the filling process.[3] Now they are filled and conduct is expected to be in some ways different. The power they contain is not less than at the Baptism, indeed it should be ever-increasing, but the power is contained and it is to be used as God directs to general edification.

Something of a parallel may be seen in the Old Testament. On one occasion the Spirit which was on Moses came upon a company of men and immediately they began to prophesy. Moses was an old vessel, well-seasoned and capable of containing power with outward calm. The others probably had to give utterance to find release— they were new vessels, and were at that time being deepened and spiritually prepared for their work. Much of the criticism which has been raised against 'Pentecost' has arisen from conduct during initial Baptisms. Indeed it first arose on the day of Pentecost—'Others mocking said, "These men are filled with new wine."' Not so! In time these men will be able to stand the same degree of power and much more without the same physical manifestations. They will learn how to walk in the new world which they have entered. All cannot be learned in an hour. Not only is a new language to be used, but also new ways of conduct adopted, with an accompanying deadness to the flesh and the 'natural' and an aliveness to God alone. But it may be asked: Do distasteful manifestations not sometimes arise even with people who are obviously sincere and anxious to obey? Now there is a difference between sincerity and a desire to obey on the one hand, and actual literal spiritual obedience on the other. One individual known to the writer was a sincere and godly man who on one occasion professed himself willing to let God do anything He desired with him. He was Irish, and in his humorous way said that he was prepared to be 'thrown over the house' if God wanted it that way. Shortly afterwards he put up a most tremendous struggle when the power of God actually came upon him. He cried out audibly, 'Not tonight, Lord, not tonight!' That is a typical case and one which was accompanied with much manifestation. There is a great difference between a person being willing to be God-controlled and the whole body and personality literally becoming so. Theory is easier than practice; the flesh dies hard in all of us—and contained in the Baptism is undoubtedly crucifixion. It can be confidently said: No distasteful manifestation ever arises when there is complete abandonment to God. But let the flesh resist, and unnecessary manifestation immediately takes place. As always, the error is in the vessel.

Now in our own day, conduct differs between waiting

meetings and normal church gatherings as it did in Paul's day; and it is to be noticed that the same criticism which is mistakenly raised today against there being more than three utterances in tongues in one meeting could have been raised about the meeting in the Upper Room. The restriction applies to regular church gatherings and not to meetings of the Upper Room type. There can be many speaking at once and that without interpretation. As ever it is necessary to distinguish between things which differ.

Thus the main theme of the chapter is conduct in the church gathering relative to the exercise of spiritual gifts. Since these gifts are spiritual, and refer to a plane of experience higher than the natural, problems insoluble to the merely natural mind inevitably arise. In the same way as the impact of the supernatural upon the natural always produces miracle, so the impact of the spiritual upon the merely intellectual always produces mystery. Nor is it always possible to explain the spiritual in terms of the natural. An attempt, however, is made in the present study to elucidate certain points which can be made intelligible to the natural mind, from a knowledge of the spiritual side of the relevant experiences. A fuller knowledge may be had only experientially.

The chapter falls into two parts:

A. *The regulation of spiritual gifts* (vv.1–33, 37–40).
B. *The conduct of women in the church* (vv.34–36).

Part *B* forms a peculiar interruption to the main theme, and has been dealt with in *A Trumpet Call to Women*; it will not be examined in detail here.

Part *A* falls into three distinct sections:

1. Various arguments against the wrong use of tongues (vv.1–25).
2. Positive instruction for the correct use of tongues, and other gifts and ministries in the church (vv.26–33).

3. The conclusion of the matter and Paul's appeal to those who are spiritual for the corroboration of his views (vv.37–40).

Section (1) falls into four sub-sections: each may be regarded as an argument against the wrong use of tongues. These arguments sometimes overlap, but their main divisions are fairly clear. Tongues without interpretation are out of order because:

(a) they leave the hearers without an understanding of their meaning (vv.1–3);
(b) such speaking is thereby unedifying to the church (vv 4–12);
(c) such speaking also prevents others in the church from participating intelligently in the spiritual exercise involved (vv.13–20);
(d) tongues were to be a sign to unbelievers. Wrongly used they defeat this end (vv.21–25).

It has not been possible to confine each section or sub-section to a uniform number of chapters. The subject matter is of unequal weight: sometimes one verse alone has required two chapters; in other cases several verses are dealt with in one chapter. In the main, the argument has been followed verse by verse, but it will be noticed that much of great value in the chapter arises as it were incidentally, as sidelights on the main theme. Some of these we will examine in depth.

The treatment is intentionally discursive. Interesting points and problems are examined as they arise. What the work loses thereby in exegetical merit it may gain in intrinsic interest.

Notes

[1] Gordon D. Fee writes of prophecy that 'it is not inherently greater, since all gifts come from the Spirit and are beneficial. It is greater precisely because it is intelligible and therefore can edify.' See Fee, *First Epistle to the Corinthians*, p.659.

2 It is not suggested that conduct in the Upper Room was mistaken. It is merely emphasised that the occasion was different and had a different purpose from normal church services. An unlimited number might there speak at once with or without interpretation and still be in order. For later church gatherings, different rules prevailed.

3 Strong physical manifestations may persist and be perfectly in order. Never despise this. As a mature vessel Kathryn Kuhlman, for example, could say that she could scarcely stand on her own feet as people were falling all around her while she ministered.

4

Follow after Love

The chapter opens with a verse which links the thought with chapter 13:

Follow after love; yet desire earnestly spiritual gifts, but rather that ye may prophesy (1 Cor 14:1).

'*Follow after love*': This link necessitates a backward digression. In chapter 13 Paul has shown love to be basic and age-enduring—unlike some, if not all, of the spiritual gifts mentioned in chapter 12, which are transitory in the sense that they pass with the advent of eternity. Unfortunately, deep misunderstanding has sometimes arisen on this subject. Special pleading has wrested things from their context, until some writers seem to be almost incapable of calm contemplation and balanced exposition. What has Paul done? In chapter 12 he has spoken of the gifts of the Spirit and indicated their usefulness in the Body of Christ. In chapter 13 he speaks of the fundamental position of 'love' for time and eternity. The Corinthians were extremely interested in the gifts, with mistaken ideas about them;[1] and rather indifferent to love, as instanced in their lawsuits with each other. Paul wanted things to be seen in proper perspective; and in placing them there he has been too often misunderstood. In no instance does he speak slightingly of the gifts, and the fact that he gives love the supreme position casts no adverse reflection whatever upon them.

From the first verse of chapter 13 some have inferred that the gifts can be exercised without 'love.' This is hardly what Paul says, nor can it be logically deduced from it. He writes: 'If I speak with the tongues of men and of angels, but have not love, I am become sounding brass, or a clanging cymbal.' The meaning of 'if' is important and later verses show the meaning. Paul supposes an individual to have what it is probably quite impossible for him to possess—the understanding of all mysteries, all knowledge, all faith. He goes on to say that even so he would be nothing if he lacked love. Now to deduce from this that it is possible to have or use these without love is logically invalid. Paul is using a common literary device and a modern example will demonstrate how illogical such an inference may be. The writer is no singer and he could say, 'If I lived to be twice as old as Methuselah, I could never sing that piece.' This does not mean that it is possible to live to such an age. An impossibility has merely been instanced to show how impossible another event is. Similarly we may not logically deduce that it was possible for people to use the gift of tongues under unction and properly, when love was absent. The sense of verse 1 in itself does not preclude such, but neither may it be inferred from it, and the whole tenor of the chapter argues for love accompanying the gifts. Now experience also teaches that these cannot be fully and properly exercised without love, and generally the deeper the love the deeper the functioning of the gift. To deduce from 1 Corinthians 13 that the gifts may be mechanically used while the soul is in a cold, loveless and backslidden state is quite mistaken. The inference is not warranted. The positions Paul mentioned were hypothetical, not actual, and the fact that they may also have been impossible is consistent with the literary device he employed to make his meaning clear. Unfortunately, confused thought on this has caused some to look almost contemptuously on the gifts and to make 'love' their quest. None ever erred in seeking 'love,' but it is too easy to be deluded into thinking that it has been found and appropriated, when in fact nothing deeper perhaps than a mere psychological experience has taken place, and then from this mistaken place to form a wrong judgment on spiritual gifts. The possession of real Christ-like love is rare in any age. One meets but few in a lifetime who bear about with them the real fragrance of Christ. Paul's exhortation to follow after love is relevant to the Church in all ages, and in ours no less than his own. But having said this, we must try to put the gifts in their proper perspective. Why does Paul list them in particular to throw love into such high relief? Simply because of their desirability and great value—in the same way as we say 'more precious than gold.' Gold is precious and by comparison with it the desirability of the preferred object is emphasised. Here gold represents the gift and love is the more desired object. Thus Paul's language, instead of downgrading the gifts, should be regarded as showing how highly desirable they are.

The fact that God has deigned to give gifts should be sufficient in itself for men to receive them with gratitude, but the more they are studied and understood, the more desirable do they become. They are to be 'desired earnestly,' Paul said. Why? Surely they were part of the Church's birthright and equipment in the war against evil. Study the effects of such powerful gifts as healing and working of miracles upon men. Notice how effective these were in Christ's own ministry and in the ministry of the apostles. They demonstrated supernatural power. Men were not left with the excuses which fill too many mouths today. There was no question of doubting the miraculous. It was too evident. Ministry was in 'the power and demonstration of the Spirit.' Can any reason be offered why such gifts should be transitory, in the sense of merely marking the beginning of the dispensation? Surely, as long as the warfare continues, the Church requires the full armoury of the gifts; and these, we know, should operate from a foundation of love. Again let me emphasise there are not two opposing ways, but two ways which lie together—the way of gift and the way of love, and these really are one way—the way of God. In our own day various parts of the world have enjoyed wonderful manifestations of the gifts of the Spirit. Healings by the thousands, conversions by the tens of thousands have taken place through those who are used in them. The need for such ministry is apparent and the warrant for it is in Scripture. Accompanying powerful gifts of healings, there is also often in operation the gift of discernment whereby wrong motives and opposing spirits are revealed. Lives become like open books and the people know that God indeed is.[2]

A glance at the list of gifts mentioned in 1 Corinthians 12:8–10 shows that none can be dispensed with: the word of wisdom, the word of knowledge, faith, gifts of healings, working of miracles, prophecy, discerning of spirits, different kinds of tongues and interpretation of tongues. All are of value and should be sought. At first it might seem that tongues do not come into the indispensable category, but a study of chapter 14 soon dispenses with that view.

Before quite leaving 1 Corinthians 13, attention should perhaps be drawn to another popular misconception which arises from verse 8 onwards:

Love never faileth: but whether there be prophecies, they shall be done away; whether there be tongues, they shall cease; whether there be knowledge, it shall be done away. For we know in part, and we prophesy in part: but when that which is perfect is come, that which is in part shall be done away . . . now we see in a mirror, darkly; but then face to face: now I know in part; but then shall I know even as also I have been known (1 Cor 13:8–10,12).

Tongues indeed shall cease: as will prophecy and knowledge. Has knowledge in the general sense (as most casual readers understand the word) ceased as yet?[3] Indeed, no! Then why should it be supposed that these others have? Surely Paul's meaning is clear. These things will cease when the 'perfect' is come.[4] The gifts indeed are transitory, in the sense that time is transitory. When the eternal age is ushered in, the gift of knowledge will no longer be required, for we shall possess knowledge. Partial sight will give place to open vision.[5] There is no shadow of an argument here for the early cessation of the miraculous gifts—tongues, prophecy and knowledge.

Finally, let me emphasise again that the 'more excellent way' of 1 Corinthians 12:31 is not a different way from the way of the gifts but merely the highest development of the same way. It does not obliterate, but includes and, including, enriches these gifts to the highest point.

Notes

[1] They were particularly interested in tongues, wisdom and knowledge. They considered themselves to be very advanced spiritually: one reason for this, as has been indicated earlier, derived from their view that when they spoke in tongues they spoke in the language of angels. They saw themselves as already sharing in heavenly life and tended to despise the body and to be indifferent to earth life.

[2] The work of the late Kathryn Kuhlman and of David Wilkerson further illustrates this type of ministry. For further reference see the author's *Reflections on the Baptism in the Holy Spirit* (New Dawn Books, 1987) and *Reflections on the Gifts of the Spirit* (New Dawn Books, 1988).

[3] On a superficial reading, knowledge may mistakenly be regarded in a general sense. Here the reference is specifically to the gift.

[4] This refers to the eternal age. There is no slightest indication that the completion of the canon of Scripture is referred to.

[5] For fuller comment on this and on 1 Corinthians 13, readers are referred to the author's *Reflections on a Song of Love* (New Dawn Books, 1988).

5

Prophecy[1]

Follow after love; yet desire earnestly spiritual gifts, but rather that ye may prophesy (1 Cor 14:1).

'. . . *but rather that ye may prophesy*': Paul shows later that one strong reason for this is that the church may be edified thereby, and the edification of the church is the dominant theme of the chapter.

Now what is prophecy?

It is not merely normal preaching but inspired utterance. It may be, and often is, of a preaching or exhortative nature. That, however, is quite a different thing from putting the matter the other way round and saying that preaching is prophesying. A study of the Greek and Hebrew words translated 'prophecy' and 'preaching' respectively, makes this abundantly clear. The word used in our chapter heading is *prophēteuō*, for which Strong gives the meanings: *to foretell events, speak under inspiration, exercise the prophetic office, prophesy.*

The words translated 'preaching' spring from quite different roots and have quite different meanings (cf. Strong):

kērussō to herald, especially divine truth (the gospel), preach, proclaim, publish, teach publicly

kērugma proclamation, preaching

euaggelizō to announce good news, preach (the gospel)

dialegomai to say thoroughly, discuss, preach unto, reason (with), speak

logos something said

In none of these cases can there be any possible confusion between prophecy and preaching. A similar distinction is maintained in the Old Testament. The idea that prophecy may be merely forth-telling has no warrant in Scripture; and to read this into it is merely to confuse the issue. Prophecy might be predictive, as in the case of Agabus, but it was not necessarily so. On the other hand, it was necessarily, and always necessarily, inspired—and this is the vital point.

Professor Peake, of commentary fame, in dealing with prophecy, may be quoted here with benefit:

> The prophets were inspired preachers; they spoke as the organs of the Holy Spirit, teaching or exhorting, but also giving new revelations or predicting the future. Paul speaks of them as reading the secrets of men's hearts, which points to a kind of clairvoyant faculty possessed and exercised by them. He appeals to this as one of the convincing signs to the outside world of God's presence in the Church. Apparently they spoke sometimes in an ecstasy. Yet the individual consciousness seems not to have been in abeyance nor the prophet to have lost the power of self-control.[2]

Far removed surely, from normal preaching![3]

'Prophecy,' Paul said, 'is to be earnestly desired.' Why? He who is used in it is used as the mouthpiece of God. How important such a ministry can be, surely needs no emphasis. It is, for example, possibly more important than the much-coveted gifts of healings, since these minister to the body, whereas prophecy ministers to the spirit.

Lest there be misconception, perhaps a further word should be said about preaching. It is my conviction that while preaching is not prophecy, all preaching ought to be under unction and not only may but should reach the fully-inspired level. To speak with less than divine authority and unction is widespread and commonly accepted, but that does not make it divinely approved. I believe preaching ought always to be God-appointed and God-anointed. Charles G. Finney was most dogmatic on this. To stand as God's representative, as the preacher is held to be, without His commission and anointing was anathema to him. The gospel, he declared, was better never preached, than preached without the power of the Holy Spirit. Otherwise it might have a hardening and harmful effect. If this is so we are not free from our brother's blood until we have taken to him life, in the power of the Spirit. Then does the word become to him a 'savour of life unto life,' or 'of death unto death' (2 Cor 2:14, AV). What a responsibility devolves upon us!

Notes

[1] This chapter closely follows the author's *Reflections on the Gifts of the Spirit*, pp.151–53.

[2] *Peake's Commentary on the Bible* (T.C. & E.C. Jack Ltd., 1920), p.647.

[3] Fee observes that 'Paul's understanding—as well as that of the other NT writers—was thoroughly conditioned by his own history in Judaism. The prophet was a person who spoke to God's people under the inspiration of the Spirit. The "inspired utterance" came by revelation and announced judgment (usually) or salvation . . . Often the word spoken had a futuristic element, so in that sense they also came to be seen as "predictors"; but that was only one element, and not necessarily the crucial one . . . the evidence in chap. 14 indicates that [prophecy] consisted of spontaneous, Spirit-inspired, intelligible messages, orally delivered in the gathered assembly,

intended for the edification or encouragement of the people. And those who prophesied were clearly understood to be "in control" (see 14:29–33)'(*First Epistle to the Corinthians*, p.595). 'By prophecy, of course, as the full evidence of this chapter makes clear, [Paul] does not mean a prepared sermon, but the spontaneous word given to God's people for the edification of the whole. Most contemporary churches would have to be radically reconstructed in terms of their self-understanding for such to take place' (*ibid.*, p.660).

6

Speaking in Tongues[1]

Verse 2 is one of the most illuminating verses in the chapter and must be read carefully:

> *For he that speaketh in a tongue speaketh not unto men, but unto God; for no man understandeth; but in the spirit he speaketh mysteries* (1 Cor 14:2).

Why '*For*'?

Paul, in his characteristic way, launches straight into his argument. He has exhorted the Corinthians to seek prophecy particularly, and is to argue later that this is more to be desired than tongues. Now the Corinthians were much more interested in tongues than in prophecy and Paul proceeds to show a certain limitation in this gift. This limitation is given as a reason why prophecy is more to be desired, and is introduced by the word *gar*, which is translated 'for' but might equally be rendered 'because.' The reason is contained briefly in the phrase: '*no man understandeth.*' The importance of this limitation in church worship is emphasised later.

'. . . *speaketh in a tongue*': The word translated 'tongue' comes from the Greek root *glōssa*, which according to

Strong means: 'the *tongue*; by implication a *language* (specifically one naturally unacquired):—tongue.'

In the Authorised Version the word 'unknown' is included before the word 'tongue' in italics. This is to indicate the nature of the 'tongue' but is not in the original text, and is omitted by the Cambridge Revisers.

Much has been written about this matter and a fair measure of agreement exists among scholars as to the nature of tongues. Differences are more pronounced in the explanation of the phenomenon and in the estimation of its value. Since much of the remainder of the chapter deals with this gift, it will not be exhaustively commented upon here. Suffice to quote from Peake and offer a few general observations.

In discussing 'tongues' and 'interpretations' he writes:

> . . . unless the person who possesses the gift of tongues possesses also the power of interpretation, not only is what he says unintelligible to the hearers but it is unintelligible also to himself. It is indeed a religious exercise in which he is engaged, his spirit prays to God, but no ideas are conveyed to the mind of the speaker; it is all incoherent rhapsody so far as he is concerned, though probably Paul would have considered that the utterances did bear an intelligible meaning in themselves (*Peake's Commentary*, pp.647–48).

And again, after discarding the views that the word 'tongue' might be taken in the physiological sense or as referring to archaic language, he writes:

> The actual utterances were probably such as we find in the magical texts, strings of words of strange formation and meaningless, but reminiscent of real, especially foreign, words . . . Possibly 1 Corinthians 13:1 pictures the form it [i.e. speaking in tongues] took, 'not as a low voiced stammering, but as shouting, sometimes dully resounding, sometimes piercing and shrill' [Harnack]. Similar phenomena . . . recur in revivalist and other movements; the Camisards and the Irvingites are well-known examples (p.648).

Various views have been put forward through the years upon the subject of tongues.

Some have maintained that the matter is straightforward. God either (a) empowered men to speak foreign languages, or (b) enabled men to understand foreign languages when they were spoken. It was a reversal of Babel, where languages were confounded. In fact, the text clearly shows that the miracle was one of speaking and not of hearing.

Others maintain that tongues were utterances given at an intense emotional pitch and might be psychologically explained in quite a natural way. Foreign words and expressions, heard perhaps in childhood and long forgotten, but still stored in the subconscious mind, might, in a deeply emotional experience, suddenly re-enter the conscious mind and be given utterance. This view had a vogue for a time, although from the first it was open to serious objections in that it did not conform to Scripture, where quite a different picture is presented. The view is now quite untenable, and that on two quite other grounds. When the view was first advanced there were possibly only a few people alive who possessed the gift of tongues and it might have been difficult always to ascertain whether they had had opportunity in childhood to hear foreign languages or not. Today the position is quite different. Millions are now in possession of the gift and innumerable cases could be given where there was no possibility of such persons having in childhood, or at any other time, heard the languages which they speak. A quite different explanation must be found.

Secondly, the emotional side has been quite distorted. Utterances in tongues are normally given without any undue emotional overtones. There certainly may be pleasurable feelings accompanying the anointing of the Spirit under which the utterances are given, but these feelings are not the controlling factor in the speaking and the phenomenon certainly cannot be explained along such lines.

Others maintain that tongues are no more than 'meaningless babble.' This certainly does not fit the miraculous experiences of the day of Pentecost, nor does it throw any light on 1 Corinthians 14. Perhaps most devastating to those who hold this view are the modern instances where tongues have been understood by hearers who happened to be naturally familiar with the languages used.[2] 'Babble' the utterances might have seemed at Pentecost to some of the hearers and even in a certain sense to the persons speaking, but to those who did understand it was wholly meaningful. When tongues were interpreted in church gatherings, there was anointed, meaningful speech between God and man.

There is a fourth group who maintain that 'tongues' and other miraculous gifts were for the beginning of the dispensation only.[3] This is held quite arbitrarily and without authority, and in the absence of any sound reason why such should be the case the view is scarcely worthy of serious consideration. It really amounts to an ignominious flight from the field of debate on the part of its exponents and it is difficult not to view it simply as a means of escaping from an embarrassing position. It should, however, perhaps be stated that history itself deals this view its deathblow. The centuries between Pentecost and the present day yield abundant evidence of the continuance of the phenomena.

To say, without authority, that such phenomena ceased either with, or before, the close of the canon of Scripture, or that since the canon is closed such phenomena are no longer to be expected, is a peculiarly foolish method of arguing. If it is maintained that the means of Baptism in the Spirit and the phenomena accompanying it have changed with the passage of time, it might as logically be said that the plan of salvation itself is now quite different from early days and that since the canon of Scripture has closed, we can expect quite new and different laws to be in operation. The position is ludicrous!

Having glimpsed even briefly these unsatisfactory views, it is difficult to understand why for so long they did have a vogue and why the sane and comparatively clear picture presented in Scripture and in 1 Corinthians 14 in particular was so long obscure to so many.

What then are Scriptural 'tongues'?

Briefly, they are an exercise of the human spirit under divine unction. They are a gift from God in a particular sense and are not merely a natural function of any part of the human body or personality. In their utterance the individual concerned is conscious of divine anointing, exceptional clarity of vision and a quickening of the mental processes. He is under no emotional strain and has a sensation of being perhaps never more alive. He is completely conscious of what is happening and is also conscious that he is not the initiator of that action. In themselves the tongues convey no meaning to his mind, although their utterance benefits him spiritually. Nor do they convey meaning to the hearers unless these happen to be naturally familiar with the language used. Tongues are often used, and rightly, when none familiar with the language is present. If the utterance is in public it is for interpretation by one with the appropriate gift; if in private, it may be left uninterpreted. The reasons for this appear later. Tongues may, of course, be used to speak directly in foreign languages to foreigners and although there is no Scriptural case of this recorded there are modern instances. In Acts 2 the understanding of tongues by foreigners seemed to be incidental. Those baptized were speaking to, or before, God and not to an audience. Whether a tongue is always a foreign earthly language or not is doubtful. 1 Corinthians 13 might seem to suggest that angelic language may be used. Indeed whether a

49

'tongue' is always or must necessarily be a language at all, has been questioned. It cannot be denied that generally the benefits to be derived by the speaker from the exercise are not much, if at all, affected by whether it is so or not. It may be argued that the spirit is engaged in a spiritual function and that whether what is spoken is understood, or capable of being understood naturally, is quite unimportant—interpretation being capable of bringing the utterance within the range of the understanding when necessary. There does not, however, seem to be any positive Scriptural warrant for the view that something other than genuine language is used.[4]

The Scriptural uses of 'tongues' may be summarised as follows:

For Prayer: 'For if I pray in a tongue, my spirit prayeth, but my understanding is unfruitful' (1 Cor 14:14).

For Praise: 'I will sing with the spirit, and I will sing with the understanding also' (1 Cor 14:15).

For Personal Edification: 'He that speaketh in a tongue edifieth himself' (1 Cor 14:4).

For a Sign to Unbelievers: 'Wherefore tongues are for a sign . . . to the unbelieving . . .' (1 Cor 14:22). Compare Mark 16:17–18: 'these signs shall follow them that believe . . . they shall speak with new tongues . . . they shall lay hands on the sick, and they shall recover.' Note that the Mark reference does not speak of the sign as exclusively for unbelievers.

For the Giving of Utterances Bearing Interpretation: 'For he that speaketh in a tongue speaketh not unto men, but unto God . . .' (1 Cor 14:2), the utterance being Godward. '. . . if I come unto you speaking with tongues, what shall I profit you, unless I speak unto you either by way of revelation, or of knowledge, or of prophesying, or of teaching?' (1 Cor 14:6), the utterance being manward.

For a Sign of the Baptism in the Spirit: 'And they of the circumcision which believed were amazed . . . because that on the Gentiles also was poured out the gift of the Holy Ghost. For they heard them speak with tongues, and magnify God' (Acts 10:46–47).[5]

Notes

[1] Substantial sections of this chapter appear in the author's *Reflections on the Baptism in the Holy Spirit*, chap. 6.

[2] See references to this, *ibid.*, pp.119–22, and also in the author's *Reflections on the Gifts of the Spirit*, pp.142, 143–44.

[3] This topic is further explored in Appendix 3.

[4] After writing the above, I discovered the following comments in Fee. In Fee's view Paul understood tongues to be 'Spirit-inspired utterance . . . not . . . out of control,' 'speech essentially unintelligible both to the speaker [1 Cor] (14:14) and to other hearers' (14:16) . . . speech directed basically toward God (14:2, 14–15, 28) (Fee, *First Epistle to the Corinthians*, p.598). 'That the Corinthians at least . . . thought of tongues as the language(s) of angels seem highly likely—for two reasons: (1) There is some evidence from Jewish sources that the angels were believed to have their own heavenly language (or dialects) and that by means of the "Spirit" one could speak these dialects . . . (2) [One] can make a good deal of sense of the Corinthian view of "spirituality" if they believed that they had already entered into some expression of angelic existence. This would explain their rejection of sexual life and sexual roles (cf. [1 Cor] 7:1–7; 11:2–16) and would also partly explain their denial of a future bodily existence (15:12, 35) . . . For them the evidence of having "arrived" at such a "spiritual" state would be their speaking the "tongues of angels." Hence the high value placed on this gift' (*ibid.*, pp.630–31).

[5] For further material on the gift of tongues, readers are referred to the author's *Reflections on the Baptism in the Holy Spirit* and *Reflections on the Gifts of the Spirit*. See also Appendix 2 below.

7

First Argument Against the Wrong Use Of Tongues

'No man understandeth'

For he that speaketh in a tongue speaketh not unto men, but unto God; for no man understandeth; but in the spirit he speaketh mysteries (1 Cor 14:2).

'. . . *speaketh not unto men but unto God*': Many are under the mistaken impression that on the day of Pentecost the baptized believers, in speaking in tongues, addressed the crowds who gathered. Hence they feel that there is a difficulty in this phrase, where men are obviously not addressed. An examination of Acts 2 in the light of 1 Corinthians 14 disposes of the problem and shows that what probably happened on that occasion was the same as has happened on innumerable occasions since. The persons baptized gave utterance in speech unintelligible to themselves but spiritually edifying. Bystanders who happened to be familiar with the languages used heard them 'speaking the mighty works of God.' Now there is no suggestion that these bystanders were directly addressed. They could have been, as has happened on the mission field in our own day. On the other hand they could equally well have been merely onlookers who happened to understand the language used in the soul's dealing with God.

Certainly there is no evidence that these disciples consciously addressed the multitude; nor did they understand the foreign languages in which they themselves spoke. To them the tongues were unknown. Christ had said that 'when he, the Spirit of Truth, is come . . . He shall glorify me: for he shall take of mine, and shall declare it unto you.' In the Baptism God the Spirit laid hold upon the human spirit[1] and tongue and through the lips of the human channel gave Christ-glorifying utterances, sometimes in tongues, sometimes in prophecy, sometimes in both. When tongues were spoken those who overheard and who knew the languages used would understand and may in an indirect way have been spoken to—but this was secondary. It should be noted again that the gift was one of utterance on the part of the believer; not, as some mistakenly think, one of hearing on the part of the audience. Thus it can be definitely said that the immediate purpose of speaking in tongues at the Baptism is not normally to give utterances intelligible to others, although this may happen. A perusal of other records of Baptisms, for example in the case of Cornelius (Acts 10) and the Ephesian twelve (Acts 19), shows that tongues were used when in all probability no foreigners were present. The immediate purpose of the Baptism is directly related to the individual concerned and not to listeners.

Thus we may say: there is no essential difference between the tongues referred to in Acts 2 and those mentioned in verse 2 of our chapter. 'He speaketh not unto men but unto God.' A very real problem, however, arises. Tongues plus interpretation, we learn later, are equivalent to prophecy, and 'he that prophesieth speaketh unto men edification and comfort and consolation'. Now if the original utterance in tongues is Godward (and verse 2 definitely envisages this), ought its interpretation not also to be Godward? That an interpretation may be manward in some cases emerges later in the chapter and will be dealt with in its own context. The Godward aspect of tongues, however, in this context is important and should not be overlooked, in view of present day practice in Pentecostal circles, where so many utterances and interpretations are manward.[2]

In this instance the individual does not speak to men, but to God. The Greek word translated 'unto' is *eis* which may bear the rendering 'before.' Thus the individual is envisaged as speaking directly to, or before, God. The speaking is not directed to man.

'. . . *for no man understandeth*': 'No man understandeth.' Let this be underlined. The hearer does not understand, nor does he require to. That the speaker is himself included in the phrase 'no man' is obvious and is further shown in later verses, verse 14 in particular, where we read: 'For if I pray in a tongue, my spirit prayeth, but my understanding is unfruitful.' We are sometimes criticised thus: 'But you don't understand what you say when you speak in tongues.' We humbly reply, 'Thank God for that. If we did, our tongues would not be Scriptural tongues.' It is as definite as that!—unpalatable as it may be to the natural and unspiritual mind! Let us accept the Word as it is, and not endeavour to force it to fit our own preconceptions. If the matter is too difficult to understand, let us wait reverently until light breaks. Better to be intellectually honest and admit inability to comprehend, than to distort the sense of the writing. If we wait with open mind, spiritual revelation may break; but if we bar the door by intellectual dishonesty, we endanger our birthright. People are generally too quick to jump to unwarranted conclusions when the sense is not at first apparent. How wise was the counsel of one old saint to me (as a boy of about twelve) about this very chapter. He was well instructed in the Scriptures, but did not understand this portion and frankly said so and in saying so pointedly added: 'There are some things you will not understand, which God will not let you understand until His own time. Wait upon him, wait for that time and all necessary revelation will surely come.' How wise was the counsel and how abundantly true! Youth wanted to know all, and too many other counsellors, who had no interpretation, made one! How different and ultimately satisfying, was the sincere 'word in season' of a mature and humble saint. Would that such advice was more generally given and perhaps followed in Christian circles. In this case light certainly did ultimately break—full, clear and unmistakable.

No, there is a mystery! Men evidently speak what, to themselves and to others, is unintelligible but, as we later learn, is also spiritually edifying.[3] Mystery upon mystery! Surely we are indeed entering the realm of the truly mystical, spiritual and supernatural. We must needs be instructed. No longer is the human spirit or human intellect the initiator of thought or activity. New realms open and new laws prevail.

'. . . *no man understandeth, but in the spirit he speaketh mysteries*': The fact, however, that 'no man understandeth' is Paul's first argument against tongues being left uninterpreted in the church. Here and throughout the chapter he argues for intelligibility in the church for the sake of the company.

'. . . *but*': Although none understands, in the Spirit mysteries are spoken. Paul seemed to recognise the difficulty to the natural mind—hence the use of 'but.' It is as though he said: 'This may seem pointless to you, *but* it has a real significance.'

'. . . *in the spirit he speaketh mysteries*': This was one of the first truths to draw me, in an intellectual sense, to Pentecost. In conjunction with the rest of the verse this sentence reveals that there is a spiritual means of expression and of communion with God, which bypasses the mind. There is a spiritual realm of existence and activity which is quite different and distinct from the natural

55

realm. Surely, I argued, since the human spirit was affected in this way in these early days, time could work no change. The needs of the human spirit in our day could hardly be different from its needs in Paul's day. The argument struck a chord within—for a definite need was felt. How often had ordinary language been found inadequate to express sorrow or joy, worship or praise. The need for tongues became apparent, and that long before they had ever been uttered or even heard by me. It is strange now to realise that this gift, whose value was appreciated before it was experienced, should be so often looked upon by some critics as useless. The very thing which in a sense drew me to Pentecost has been a point of difficulty and controversy for so many others. How true and terrible a reflection this casts upon the unspiritual outlook of our age. It reminds one of the story of the ignorant critic of the old masters. 'Sir,' said the gallery attendant, 'it is not they who are on trial. It is you.' So with tongues and their value! They are not on trial. It is their critics who are in the dock. Needless to say, the value anticipated in the gift has been much more than realised. It has proved all it gave promise of being.[4]

Notes

[1] When Paul said he would pray with the spirit in verse 15, Fee defines him as meaning 'by means of the Holy Spirit through [his] spirit' (*First Epistle to the Corinthians*, p.666).

[2] There is no question that when an utterance in tongues is Godward so must its interpretation be. Some of the most wonderful interpretations I have ever heard have been of this kind. They have been veritable paeans of inspired praise.

[3] Fee writes: 'The edifying of oneself is not self-centeredness, but the personal edifying of the believer that comes through private prayer and praise. Although one may wonder how "mysteries" that are not understood even by the speaker can

edify, the answer lies in vv. 14–15. Contrary to the opinion of many, spiritual edification can take place in ways other than through the cortex of the brain. Paul believed in an immediate communing with God by means of the S/spirit that sometimes bypassed the mind; and in vv.14–15 he argues that for his own edification he will have both.' *First Epistle to the Corinthians*, p.657.

[4] See Appendix 2.

8

Second Argument

The unedifying nature of uninterpreted tongues

But he that prophesieth speaketh unto men edification, and comfort, and consolation (1 Cor 14:3).

Why '*But*'? We have seen what tongues in themselves are. Their usefulness is limited, 'but,' says Paul in other words, 'observe what happens when one prophesies.' The underlying thought and purpose in his mind is to show the usefulness of prophecy in the church, for edification; and the comparative uselessness of uninterpreted tongues, to this end. It appears later that when these are interpreted the combined gifts of tongues and interpretation are equal in value to prophecy. Almost the whole purpose of the chapter is to regulate the use of the gifts of tongues, interpretation and prophecy in the church and to do so, Paul first of all indicates their functions and usefulness. Their scope and value for edification decide their place in the public service.

It appears that almost all types of vocal spiritual instruction may be included in prophecy. The prophet speaks edification, comfort and consolation. Notice the scope of the word 'edification.' It may include exhortation or rebuke. Some have questioned the inclusion of rebuke, but surely it is a fundamental and permanent spiritual principle that evil must be rebuked and dealt with before certain positive upbuilding can take place. The destroying process may be regarded as a stage in the upbuilding or edifying. The predictive element which may be in prophecy is not indicated here.

Many hold the view that there is a difference between the prophets referred to in Ephesians, for example—who were gifts of Christ to the church—and the ordinary prophets whose gift is spoken of in this verse. The first are regarded as much greater than the latter. This cannot, however, be maintained from the absence of the predictive element in this verse, for later in the chapter the revealing and discerning elements in the gift are disclosed. It is sometimes argued from the text, 'Let all prophesy,' that this obviously envisages a more numerous class than that to which the prophets of Ephesians belonged. But surely 'all' were 'all with the gift'—perhaps relatively few in a normal meeting. It seems to me that there is no clear distinction. Perhaps Agabus was greater than some of those with the gift of prophecy in Corinth, but that could have been a difference of degree rather than of kind. Note the absence of personal and private direction in the list of the functions of prophecy indicated here. Personal direction has become such a controversial subject that it has been given an appendix of its own.[1]

He that speaketh in a tongue edifieth himself; but he that prophesieth edifieth the church (1 Cor 14:4).

The practice against which Paul is writing must be constantly remembered. It is continually in his mind and again and again he reverts to his dominant theme. The Corinthians seem to have been in the habit of speaking much in tongues. Possibly many spoke at one time and that without interpretation. Possibly they had reached a sort of half-way position between the practice of the day of Pentecost and the regulated position towards which Paul was directing them. Their practice, Paul taught, was not to general edification and must stop. No longer are they to be as babes. They are to grow and develop and so are their spiritual functions. Line by line, Paul shows them the superior merits of prophecy as compared with tongues, unless the latter are interpreted and give intellectual enlightenment. He expects spiritual conduct to improve.

It should be noted that Paul's assault is never on 'tongues' as some have imagined, but on 'uninterpreted tongues' in the public gathering of the church. This is the main argument and it dominates most of the chapter.

It is interesting to note the wealth of information that may be gleaned about the gifts and spiritual principles generally, as sidelights that are almost incidental to the main argument are cast upon them. We notice, for example, that the person speaking in a tongue edifies himself. We have already noticed that he does not understand what he says when speaking in tongues. Now we have it emphasised that, despite this, he is edified by so speaking. Passing strange to the natural mind! He neither understands, nor do his fellows; yet he is spiritually built up. This problem is further examined in chapter 10 below. The unedifying nature of uninterpreted tongues to the company generally, constitutes Paul's second argument against the abuse. The theme continues to verse 15.

Now I would have you all speak with tongues, but rather that ye should prophesy; and greater is he that prophesieth than he that speaketh in tongues, except he interpret, that the church may receive edifying (1 Cor 14:5).

'. . . *that the church may receive edifying*': This phrase gives the keynote of the chapter. Paul may be paraphrased as saying: 'You speak much in tongues in Corinth. I am glad. I would like you all to speak in tongues, but I would rather have you prophesying; for the person speaking in prophecy is greater than the person who speaks in tongues, unless the latter interprets, because only then is the church edified, and what you do publicly in the church must be for public, not private benefit.'

The critical phrase is: '*except he interpret*.'[2] Paul wanted all to speak in tongues, but he wanted none to do so unless these were interpreted, in which case the combined gifts, tongues and interpretation, would become equal to prophecy. This becomes clearer later.

> *But now, brethren, if I come unto you speaking in tongues, what shall I profit you, unless I speak to you either by way of revelation, or of knowledge, or of prophesying, or of teaching?* (1 Cor 14:6)[3]

This is a vital verse. It is the only verse in Scripture which gives the suggestion that the interpretation of tongues may be manward. Paul has reiterated the theme that tongues without interpretation are out of order. He amplifies this here and maintains that it would be profitless for him to come amongst them speaking in tongues alone. The church was to be edified and 'how,' he asks, 'will you be edified unless I speak to you by way of revelation or of knowledge or of prophesying or of teaching?' In other words, these come through interpretation, and any or all may be contained in interpretation. This is of great significance, and may be easily missed if the dominant line of Paul's argument is not closely followed.

To understand the significance more clearly let us recapitulate: Paul puts tongues on one side and prophecy on the other and shows the superior merits of the latter. He then shows the comparative uselessness of the former, unless joined to the sister gift of interpretation, in which case the combined gifts are equal to prophecy. Thus he declares that if he merely comes to the Corinthians speaking in tongues he shall not profit them unless he speaks also by way of revelation or of knowledge or of prophesying or of teaching, in which case he would be obeying his own injunction in having the tongue interpreted—these things being contained in interpretation.

That tongues may have a Godward interpretation is clearly seen in verse 2, but verse 6 alone gives clear Scriptural precedent for the general practice in Pentecostal circles of having manward interpretation. It is evident from this passage that men were directly addressed in the interpretation. Hence the utterance in tongues would also be manward, although in itself unintelligible. Elsewhere tongues are generally regarded as Godward as, for example, in verse 2. Hence the vital significance of this verse should not be overlooked. With the exception of verse 19, on which comment will be made later, it stands on its own in the New Testament.

Finally, notice the great scope of the gift of interpretation. Its importance needs no emphasis, particularly when we bear in mind that everything included in prophecy is included again here.

Revelation is discussed in chapter 14 when verse 30 is considered.

Notes

[1] Appendix 4.

[2] Fee writes: 'The interpretation of the tongue brings it within the framework of intelligibility, which in turn means that it too can edify the community. This does not imply that such a tongue is to be understood as directed toward the community, but that what the person has been speaking to God has now been made intelligible, so that others may benefit from the Spirit's utterance.' Fee, *First Epistle to the Corinthians*, p.659.

[3] Fee has an interesting observation on teaching: 'Equally intriguing is the appearance of "teaching," which corresponds to "the teacher" in 12:28 as prophecy does to the prophet. Probably this has to do with a Spirit-inspired utterance that took the form of instruction, rather than with the more common usage that implies formal teaching of some kind . . . how this differs in terms of content from the other items on this list is a matter of speculation since the data are so meager.' *Ibid.*, p.663.

9

Second Argument Continued

The pointlessness of uninterpreted tongues

Even things without life, giving a voice, whether pipe or harp, if they give not a distinction in the sounds, how shall it be known what is piped or harped? For if the trumpet give an uncertain voice, who shall prepare himself for war? So also ye, unless ye utter by the tongue speech easy to be understood, how shall it be known what is spoken? for ye will be speaking into the air.[1] There are, it may be, so many kinds of voices in the world, and no kind is without signification. If then I know not the meaning of the voice, I shall be to him that speaketh a barbarian, and he that speaketh will be a barbarian unto me. So also ye, since ye are zealous of spiritual gifts, seek that ye may abound unto the edifying of the church (1 Cor 14:7–12).

These verses continue Paul's second attack upon the practice of having tongues without interpretation and are in themselves a minor sub-division of the argument. He first argued that tongues were not addressed to men (v.2). Secondly, they were unedifying to the gathering (v.4), and now he further demonstrates how their unintelligible nature renders them pointless. The arguments are interwoven—this is really a continuation and amplification of the second. A third comes later when Paul shows how impossible it is for the congregation to take any meaningful part in uninterpreted tongues. 'Else if thou bless with the Spirit, how shall he that filleth the place of the unlearned say the Amen at thy giving of thanks, seeing he knoweth not what thou sayest (v.16)?' The fourth shows that tongues intended as a sign to unbelievers, wrongly used, defeat their own end. This concludes Paul's attack on the abuse.

These verses must be viewed in their immediate context. When this is done they are seen to fit into the general argument exactly. Too often they have been wrested out of context and foolishly used as a weapon against the gift of tongues. Tracts and books have appeared with such titles as 'Why be a barbarian?' with the suggestion that one is reverting to such a state, if one speaks in tongues. The suggestion is made that tongues generally are mere gibberish and that genuine tongues must have been known languages—which were, however, not to be spoken unless generally understood. All sorts of fanciful suggestions have been made and often a phrase or argument has been culled from these verses without even the semblance of regard for the context and then used as justification for such views.

Viewed properly, the verses present no difficulty whatever. They are simply a continuation of the attack upon the abuse. It is strange how persistently Paul reverts to this same point. It would almost appear that the Corinthians were deeply-rooted in the opinion that the mere utterance of tongues was in itself a beneficial exercise for the whole assembly. Paul is not satisfied with simply denying this. He reiterates his denial again and again and systematically builds his case against the view. Indeed, it is the strength and insistence of his argument against the abuse which may have given some the impression that he belittles tongues altogether. Such a view is quite mistaken. The attack is ever and always upon the abuse, never upon the use or usefulness of the gift. Tongues, rightly used, were always to be encouraged.

The last verse of this group again strikes the keynote of the chapter: 'Seek that ye may abound to the edifying of the church.'[2]

Wherefore let him that speaketh in a tongue pray that he may interpret (1 Cor 14:13).

The exhortation to 'abound to the edifying of the church' has been given. This verse shows one way in which it may be done, namely, by having tongues interpreted. The verse also concludes the foregoing section, and is simply a reiteration of what Paul has been saying all through.

'. . . *let him* . . . *pray that he may interpret*': This is conclusive in the argument that the person speaking in a tongue has no understanding of what he himself says. If he did understand, he would have no need to pray for interpretation. The fact that he requires to do so clearly demonstrates that tongues were not understood.

This verse is also a conclusive answer to those who regard tongues as merely languages with which the speaker is naturally familiar. In the light of the whole chapter, this view is almost too ludicrous to be seriously considered. However, it runs as follows: Corinth was a cosmopolitan city and probably people of various languages were found in the church. Paul was legislating for the way in which these people were to take part in the services. If a language was not known generally, a person with that language was not to speak in it unless he could interpret (in which case his speaking in it in the first instance seems rather pointless) or unless someone else in the gathering could interpret (i.e. through a natural knowledge of the language used).

According to this view, the miraculous element is shorn from both tongues and interpretation, which, of course, is completely out of line with the whole sense of the chapter. Indeed, any view which regards tongues as natural and intelligible to the speaker cannot be maintained in the light of the clear statement in this passage.

Others who regard 'tongues' as foreign languages known to the speaker but interpretation as a spiritual gift must be careful not to deny the miraculous in tongues merely to admit it in interpretation. One finds difficulty or rather embarrassment in commenting on some of the views which the opponents of Pentecost have put forward. These are so often found to be structurally weak and in many cases completely untenable.

The sense in this case is plain! The verse says: 'Wherefore let him that speaketh in a tongue pray that he may interpret.' The 'tongue' is given by divine inspiration and from the same source must the interpretation come. Both utterances are spiritual—the product of spiritual gifts—and neither may be regarded as a normal function of the human spirit or mind.

Notice the word 'interpretation'. The word is not 'translation' and an interpretation is not necessarily a translation.[3] In ordinary life, different people may witness the same event and, according to their different types, give different interpretations of it. Types vary, and as they vary, so do their interpretations. A passage of English literature may be interpreted in two words or in two thousand. It can be interpreted generally, superficially, or exhaustively. The interpretation will tend to vary according to the character, understanding, ability and insight of the reader. So it is in the spiritual realm. A 'tongue' is a spiritual utterance and the interpretation of the utterance is spiritual. Thus the depth and quality of these may well be affected by the spiritual maturity of the persons through whom they come. This does not make them any the less accurate nor does it reflect on their divine origin. In the Bible itself we see differences in types of expression amongst various writers. For example, John's writings bear features peculiar to himself, and different in type from Mark's. When the former are examined the same construction of sentence may be seen again and again and not anywhere else in the New Testament. This in no way impairs the accuracy of John's writing or its full inspiration—nor does it reflect adversely on Mark's writing. God pours Himself through men, according to their types. One reason for the great need for Christians to grow deep spiritually is simply that God may be able to use them deeply. More than truth is involved in a message from God to man. Power, depth and fulness are all affected and shallowness in a channel can greatly hinder God's purpose. Instead of a deep, spiritually rich utterance being given, a lighter and less penetrating (albeit true and accurate) message may be delivered. Thus inspiration is not a mere mechanical process in which the inspired vessel has no part whatever. There is undoubtedly a relation between the utterance, whether spoken or written, and the channel through whom it comes.

In practice, the gift of interpretation seems to function differently through different channels. With some, interpretation is received as a series of pictures; others find thought illumined and directed and themselves borne along as a ship by the wind. Others again have the impression of reading unfolding lines as from a page. The means of operation may vary but the gift is the same and it can happen that two people in whom the working is different receive exactly the same message. It should be emphasised that interpretations often are exactly the same—several receiving and one giving forth.[4] The foregoing is merely to show that this is not necessarily so.

Notes

1 Fee writes: 'Tongues, Paul is arguing, is like the harpist running fingers over all the strings, making musical sounds but not playing a pleasing melody, or like a bugler who blows the bugle without sounding the battle cry. In both cases sounds come from the instrument, but they make no sense; hence they do not benefit the listener. So it is with tongues.' *First Epistle to the Corinthians*, p.664.

2 Fee comments: 'In a time when charismatic utterances are experiencing something of a revival in the church, this paragraph is especially important to those in that renewal. The point of everything in corporate worship is not personal experience in the Spirit, but building up the church itself. Much that comes under the banner of charismatic or pentecostal worship seems very often to fail right at this point. However, it is not so much that what goes on is not understood by the others, but that it fails to have this final verse as its basic urgency. The building up of the community is the basic reason for corporate settings of worship; they should probably not be turned into a corporate gathering for a thousand individual experiences of worship.' *Ibid.*, p.667.

3 According to Fee, 'Although this term could mean something close to "translation," it can also mean "to put into words"; in this context [1 Cor 12:10] it probably means to articulate for the benefit of the community what the tongues-speaker has said. The evidence from 14:5, 13 and 27–28 indicates (a) that this, too, is a "Spirit-inspired" gift of utterance, and (b) that it may be given either to the tongues-speaker or to another' (*ibid.*, pp.598–99).

4 In international gatherings two or more may interpret one utterance in tongues, one after the other, for the benefit of the various nationalities represented. Hence the accuracy of the interpretations can be tested. This has actually happened, with amazing results. Accuracy has been abundantly demonstrated. Reports of such occurrences may be found from time to time in the publications of various Pentecostal groups.

10

Second Argument Concluded

For if I pray in a tongue, my spirit prayeth, but my understanding is unfruitful (1 Cor 14:14).

Here is clear evidence, clearly reiterated, that Scriptural tongues leave the mind of the person using them without understanding of what is said. The bewildered cry: 'What then is the use of them?' is indeed a sad reflection on our western civilization, so long misled by mistaken and now largely discarded philosophic assumptions. The human mind has so long and so wrongly been enthroned that it is still difficult even for those who are well aware of the old fallacies to be quite free from their pernicious influence and to strike a correct balance in their judgments. It is gradually and increasingly emerging, however, that 'mind' is not the arbiter of action in man, but is itself subject to deeper underlying forces in personality[1], its decisions being often conditioned and determined by these. It is interesting in this connection to recall that a number of British professors of philosophy once met and were astounded to realise that their philosophic views varied according to their psychological types. Where they had felt that their systems of thought had sprung more or less from pure reason, that these were unbiased and the result of calm judgment, it appeared that all along they had been, to some extent at least, duped by deeper underlying forces in their own personalities—which forces were predisposing them to certain lines of thought. No doubt their views may have been honest, but they were still conditioned views. It is precisely with this deep submerged part in human personality that God deals, and in association with which spiritual gifts function. God desires truth and cleanness in the inner parts and when man is right, he tends to think right. Mind indeed was never meant to be the master, but rather the servant of the soul. Strangely too, or perhaps not so strangely, mind itself reaches its highest attainment and clarity when it is denied paramount place and is allowed to function under the control of the Spirit, unctioned by God.

Thus in the functioning of the gifts of the Spirit, such as interpretation and prophecy, the mind is in a sense passive so far as normal thought processes are concerned and active only in the sense that it is open Godward, and yet in this passive state its power and perception are infinitely higher than when it is given the primary and active role.[2] This, however, to most people is a mystery and to a Church still suffering from the backwash of dreadfully mistaken naturalistic philosophy, spiritual edification, in which the mind has not the initiating part, is as yet difficult to comprehend. And yet this is so clearly in line with the fundamental principles of our whole religion. Christianity is a miraculous and supernatural religion. It is founded upon miracle, continues and grows in miracle. Never is there a soul born into the Kingdom nor an advance made in the things of the Kingdom, apart from miracle; and in these things the spirit is in the ascendant with mind functioning in a controlled and secondary role. Thus the cry, 'What is the use of tongues?' is in reality a profound reflection on the naturalism and materialism

71

which have affected a once spiritual Church. It is a confession of spiritual bankruptcy and poverty.

'. . . *if I pray in a tongue*': This shows that prayer is one of the various uses of tongues, as indicated earlier. In such prayer the person does not understand the meaning of the words he uses.

'. . . *my spirit prayeth*': This is why he does not understand.[3] It is a spiritual exercise in which he is engaged and one in which the understanding has no part. This at first seems difficult but reflection helps to make it understandable.

Surely sorrow, joy, love, anxiety are primarily things of the spirit, rather than things of the mind—they make a wordless impact upon the spirit. They are felt without any active mental process being involved. Sometimes it is impossible to express them in words at all even if desired. Thus it can be with a burden of prayer. The pressure is upon the spirit. It is felt. Words may fail to express it. Indeed the very effort to find words may in itself prove a distraction. The framing of language decreases the spiritual concentration and it is here that 'tongues' can be of great value. By their use, the concentration can be focused upon God Himself, or upon the object indicated, and the whole spirit pour itself out without language distraction; thus the burden lifts and the work is accomplished without the interference of mind, which in any case does not have a primary role in such matters. Surely this gift is a powerful weapon in the Church's armoury!

Something of a parallel in a different sphere may be found in the effect of music upon the human spirit. Music can, without any active intellectual accompaniment, move the spirit to joy and happiness, sorrow and sadness. These are states of soul and when the state is one of need for prayer, or spiritual burden for others, 'tongues' can meet that need. Music does not affect the understanding. Neither do tongues. Yet they both meet a need and effect a purpose. When music is so welcome why should tongues be shunned and regarded as irrational?

> *What is it then? I will pray with the spirit, and I will pray with the understanding also: I will sing with the spirit, and I will sing with the understanding also* (1 Cor 14:15).[4]

We are not, however, in private here. The church meeting is not for private but for public edification and usefulness, and prayer is to be interpreted that others may share in it. The word 'spirit' here is equated with the word 'tongue,' and the word 'understanding' with the word 'interpretation.' This is important and is only fully appreciated if the main argument is closely followed.

The verse reveals a further use of tongues. Not only may prayer be in tongues—so also may singing, and such singing is to be interpreted.[5]

The fact that the word 'spirit' is used of one exercise and 'understanding' of the other, does not mean that 'spirit' may not be included in 'understanding' although the second is not *necessarily* in the first. That it is in fact included appears later; but we should note at this point that an interpretation is fully as deep an utterance in the spirit as is tongues, but in the case of interpretation the understanding also plays a part—not that it controls, but it is used and enlightened and has a knowing part in what takes place; whereas when tongues are used the understanding is completely quiescent.

Notes

[1] See Appendix 1.
[2] See Appendix 5.
[3] According to Fee, 'in the present context the difficult wording "my spirit prays" seems to mean something like "my S/spirit prays." On the one hand, both the possessive "my" and the contrast with "my mind" indicate that he is here referring to

his own "spirit" at prayer. On the other hand, there can be little question, on the basis of the combined evidence of 12:7–11 and 14:2 and 16, that Paul understood speaking in tongues to be an activity of the Spirit in one's life; it is prayer and praise directed toward God in the language of Spirit-inspiration. The most viable solution to this ambiguity is that by the language "my spirit prays" Paul means his own spirit is praying as the Holy Spirit gives the utterance. Hence, "my S/spirit prays."' Fee, *First Epistle to the Corinthians*, p.670.

[4] Fee writes *ibid.*: 'As v.15 makes certain, Paul does not mean that praying in the Spirit is a bad thing because it does not benefit his understanding; rather, this states the way things are. What he does go on to say is that he will do *two* things—one apparently for his own sake, the other for the sake of others.'

[5] I personally favour congregational singing in tongues—although this is not mentioned in Scripture. It can be very beautiful indeed. Its harmonies, one feels, are out of this world, and it can have a profound spiritual effect. I never cease to wonder at the wonderful control exercised on a large company without any human leading, and at how the singing normally ceases suddenly as though everyone is moved at exactly the same moment.

When individuals speak to themselves and to God in tongues, as distinct from speaking aloud in utterances for interpretation, an undertone of sound may ensue. To my mind this is in order. Similarly a whole company can sing, and this is recognisably different from a person singing a solo in tongues which is obviously for interpretation. The two situations are parallel and neither breaks Scriptural injunction.

11

Third Argument

Uninterpreted tongues preclude the church's participation

Else if thou bless with the spirit, how shall he that filleth the place of the unlearned say the Amen at thy giving of thanks, seeing he knoweth not what thou sayest? For thou verily givest thanks well, but the other is not edified (1 Cor 14:16–17).

Again the pressing of the same line of argument. Tongues are to be interpreted. The equating of the word 'spirit' with the word 'tongue' is obvious. Prayer has been instanced earlier as one use of tongues. Now 'prayer' is a word with a wide connotation. Within it may be included the making of requests (general and public, or personal and particular), praise and thanksgiving. 'Blessing' seems to be synonymous with 'praise.' While we are not told earlier which particular type of prayer took place when tongues were employed, we can certainly say from this verse that blessing may be included. Hence in the interpretation of such an utterance, the address will be Godward, as the utterance is Godward, and will be of a praise-and-thanksgiving nature.

'. . . *the unlearned*': Does this mean the congregation generally? 'Unlearned' simply because the utterance is in tongues? or is Paul's reference more specifically to those who do not happen to be learned by education or experience and so are unacquainted with the language used?

There are two alternatives: First, a comparison with verse 31 shows that with the proper use of prophecy 'all may learn.' With the improper use of tongues the congregation generally does not learn. Thus the unlearned will really include all who do not have the interpretation by divine illumination and who therefore cannot conscientiously say the 'Amen' at the end of the utterance. They simply do not understand the language used and are left 'unlearned' because the utterance is not interpreted. Having no understanding of it they are thereby left unedified. It is precisely against this that Paul writes. If and when the interpretation comes, they in turn will learn what is said and will be able to say the 'Amen.'

Secondly, the view may be adopted that Paul here specifically refers to those who have not deeply studied and are unacquainted with a wide range of languages. (This would probably include most of the assembly.) Although the tongue spoken is not understood by the speaker, or by the congregation generally, it would, of course, be understood in a natural way by a person who happened to be familiar with the language used—as happened, for example, at Pentecost and has often been repeated since. Such a person, learned in the language, could easily say the 'Amen' at such giving of thanks.

From the general argument Paul certainly seems to have had the mass of the congregation in mind, and the word 'unlearned' may well include all who neither receive the interpretation by divine revelation, nor receive it through the use of that gift, nor happen to be familiar with the language used.[1]

I thank God, I speak with tongues more than you all (1 Cor 14:18).[2]

Here speaks the great apostle of the Gentiles. Notice the tense used: 'I speak'—not, 'I used to speak,' as a young and immature believer. Surely if the gift was primitive, transitory and comparatively valueless such a spiritual giant as Paul would long since have discarded it. And mark what a giant the man was—as organiser, missionary, evangelist, mystic and writer. Head and shoulders above his brethren in so many spheres!—'I speak in tongues more than you all.'[3]

How comforting it has frequently been in facing the criticism of our sometimes deeply spiritual but, alas, often sadly mistaken brethren, to realise that were Paul himself and the other apostles alive in our midst, they would indubitably be numbered with the 'tongues people.' Again let it be emphasised: the Church generally in our day is not greater or more enlightened than was the early Church. The movement has been markedly in the other direction. When, if ever, the Church approximates to the standing of the early Church she will find that again the power and the spiritual gifts of a former age will be manifest in her midst. In that hour she will be a Church indeed—a place of salvation, healing, exorcism and miracle; in short, she will be what she was intended to be—a divine and supernatural institution working the works of God in a lost world.

This is the only place where we read that Paul spoke in tongues and this is of great importance since in the cases in the New Testament in which it is stated that individuals or companies were baptized in, or filled with, the Spirit, as Paul was, it is also stated that they spoke in tongues, with two exceptions: (1) the case of Paul—and here we learn that he spoke in tongues more than all the Corinthians; and (2) the case of the Samaritans—and in that instance we read that Simon Magus desired the ability to 'lay on hands' that others might receive the Holy Spirit—for he saw that by this means the Spirit was given. It seems certain therefore that there was some outward manifestation of the reception of the Spirit by the Samaritans.

Thus we reach the conclusion that in every case there was an outward and definite manifestation of the inward experience and that possibly tongues were always in evidence, although this is not categorically stated. We should also remember that the manifestation was not itself the experience but was produced by it.

Howbeit in the church I had rather speak five words with my understanding that I might instruct others also, than ten thousand words in a tongue (1 Cor 14:19).[4]

This verse really reverts to the general theme of the second argument. Again the same line is pressed, but how often and how grievously has this verse been wrested from its context. Paul is still insisting on the same point. In the church there is to be 'understanding' for general edification. Tongues alone do not give this. 'Therefore,' says Paul, 'I would rather speak five words *with my understanding* in the church that I might instruct others also, than ten thousand words in a tongue.' The 'tongue' means, of course, an uninterpreted tongue. Without this understanding the whole verse loses its meaning and significance. It was precisely to emphasise the point that others should receive benefit that the verse and most of the chapter were written. The ten thousand words would, by interpretation, pass into the realm of the understanding and thus edify the church. The attack, again, is not upon tongues, but upon tongues which are left uninterpreted.

It is remarkable how determinedly and persistently Paul manages to bring his main theme and argument into almost every single verse. And for the reader to lose sight of the main theme is to put him in danger of grave misinterpretation, as has too often happened, and too often with this particular verse.

Note the use of the word 'instruct.' The underlying idea is that tongues are to be interpreted: ten thousand words in an uninterpreted tongue would not give instruction; interpreted, they would. There is also contained in this at least the suggestion of the manward side in interpretation. Secondly, there is an overtone which could relate to women. If a prophetess does the interpreting, she is seen as giving instruction.

> *Brethren, be not children in mind: howbeit in malice be ye babes, but in mind be men* (1 Cor 14:20).[5]

Paul appears to judge the Corinthians' attitude to uninterpreted tongues as 'childish' and exhorts them to grow into manhood. In the foregoing verses he has indicated the way to maturity of outlook and practice so far as the function of the gift of tongues is concerned.

This verse concludes a distinct section of the chapter.

Notes

[1] Fee writes: 'Paul's description of the person who cannot say the "Amen," however, is puzzling: (literally) "the one who fills the place of the *idiotes*." The problem is twofold: (1) whether the expression "fills the place of" is to be taken literally or figuratively; and (2) what *idiotes* itself means here. The problem is complicated by two factors: (a) Although the word ordinarily means "nonexpert," hence "an ordinary person" in contrast to one who is skilled, there is also evidence that it was a technical term in religious life for nonmembers who still participated in the pagan sacrifices. (b) In the present context this same person in v.17 is referred to as being "built up," which in Paul has to do with believers, yet the word *idiotes* reappears in v.23 in close connection with unbelievers.' See Fee, *First Epistle to the Corinthians*, p.672. In a note on p.673, he also comments, 'The issue is . . . between intelligibility and [the gift of tongues] in the assembly. Even other tongues-

speakers will be *idiotes* in the sense that Paul is using the word, since they, too, will be unable to understand what is being said by the others.'

2 Fee writes: 'If our suggestion has been correct, that there is an undercurrent of apologetic in these references, where Paul is both defending his own status with regard to their criterion—the gift of tongues—and rejecting their use of it, then these sentences are intended to fall like something of a bombshell in Corinth. Despite what they may think, he can assert—with thanksgiving to God!—"I speak in tongues more than all of you." His concern throughout has been with uninterpreted tongues in the assembly, because they cannot edify the church. With this sentence he outmaneuvers the Corinthians altogether. He herewith affirms their gift in the strongest of terms; but he does so in order to reorder their own thinking about what was going on in the assembly.' *Ibid.*, p.675.

3 Dean Farrar wrote: 'Paul as he stands in the light of history; Paul as he is preserved for us in the records of Christianity; Paul energetic as Peter, and contemplative as John; Paul the hero of unselfishness; Paul the mighty champion of spiritual freedom; Paul a greater preacher than Chrysostom, a greater missionary than Xavier, a greater reformer than Luther, a greater theologian than St. Thomas of Aquinum; Paul the inspired Apostle of the Gentiles, the slave of the Lord Jesus Christ' (F.W. Farrar, *The Life and Work of St. Paul* [Cassell, n.d.], p.7).

This is the man who said: 'I thank God I speak in tongues more than you all.'

4 Fee writes: 'In church "five intelligible words" are to be pre-ferred to "ten thousand words in a tongue." Only the language for edification has changed: "to instruct others." ' Again, 'this . . . needs to be heard well by those on both sides of the "tongues issue." Those who tend to discount it as meaningful because of Paul's strong words against it in the assembly need to pay closer attention to his own determination to pray and praise in this way—and his thanksgiving for it. On the other side, those who have rediscovered this gift as a meaningful expression in their personal lives of devotion need to be especially conscious of the greater concern of this paragraph that the gathered assembly be a time for the building up of others

individually and the body as a whole.' (Fee, *First Epistle to the Corinthians*, pp.675–76).

5 This verse should be compared with 1 Corinthians 13:11, where Paul says, 'When I was a child, I spake as a child, I felt as a child, I thought as a child: now that I am become a man, I have put away childish things.' Paul went on speaking in tongues when he was a mature man. The childishness here does not refer to using the gift of tongues but to abusing it—in having tongues left uninterpreted when publicly uttered.

12

Fourth Argument

Tongues are a 'sign to unbelievers'; wrongly used they defeat that end.

In the law it is written, By men of strange tongues and by the lips of strangers will I speak unto this people; and not even thus will they hear me, saith the Lord (1 Cor 14:21).

This commences a section of considerable difficulty. Indeed many have felt that definite contradiction is contained in the following verses. This, however, is not so and a careful study of each verse makes Paul's meaning plain.

The quotation is from Isaiah 28:11–12 and the slight variations in language may be accounted for by the use of the Septuagint Version.

One main question arises: in what way was 'this people' to be spoken to by 'men of strange tongues' and 'the lips of strangers'? Was it directly in a way that they would understand, through foreigners speaking their language, as probably Old Testament commentators thought, or was it in quite another and supernatural way? That it was the latter soon emerges.

'. . . *not even thus will they hear me*': Despite such supernatural manifestation the Jews generally would not accept God's voice. Even in our own day the manifestation of divine power in the realm of the miraculous does not cause

all to turn to God. When the heart is not right with God,
nor prepared to be right, the witnessing of miracle in itself
may produce no change. Intellectual conviction is not as
important as surrendered will. Thus the manifestation of
the divine presence, through this supernatural gift of the
Spirit, was not destined to turn Israel to God.

> *Wherefore tongues are for a sign, not to them that believe,
> but to the unbelieving: but propheysing is for a sign, not to
> the unbelieving, but to them that believe* (1 Cor 14:22).

The first sentence answers the question of the preceding
verse. The people are spoken to by a sign—a supernatural
sign. There are various ways in which man may be spoken
to other than by a direct voice: for example, by circum-
stance or through inner conviction. In this case, they are
spoken to by a sign—the sign of tongues, and the speaking is indirect.

The use of this gift, or this sign, in early days, seems to
have made a deep impression upon unbelievers—convinc-
ing many of the supernatural presence of God. A similar
impression is still often produced in our own day, when
the same gift is rightly used. It has often been noticed that
the reaction of unbelievers to tongues is markedly different from that of certain prejudiced sections of believers.
Young unbiased converts also are remarkably attracted by
the gifts of the Spirit and, when properly instructed, generally enter quickly into real Pentecostal experience. It is
important too that this should take place before the cool-
ing process (which often begins soon after conversion) sets
in. If a convert is quickly baptized in the Spirit he may
maintain the spiritual glow indefinitely.

Now the sign is to the 'unbelieving' not the 'believing.'
Prophecy, however, is a sign to the 'believing' not to the
'unbelieving.' Is there again the suggestion of the same
underlying thought in Paul's mind—the superiority of

prophecy to tongues in themselves? Prophecy was for the mature believer, whereas tongues as a sign was for the unbeliever, and in so far as the believer was more important (in one sense) than the unbeliever, so was prophecy more important than uninterpreted tongues. Now in what way is prophecy a sign to the believer? How often one has become aware of the presence of God in an assembly when some God-anointed prophet has risen to minister. True prophecy is always a sign to the believer of the divine presence and apart from divine presence cannot be given. It is, in addition, peculiarly a means whereby God addresses and instructs His own.

If therefore the whole church be assembled together, and all speak with tongues, and there come in men unlearned or unbelieving, will they not say that ye are mad? (1 Cor 14:23).

Paul now shows what the effect on the unbelievers will be—not by use, but by abuse of tongues. Not only will they not be spoken to by them, in the intended 'sign' way, but they will accuse those speaking of being mad. Notice the phrase 'If . . . all speak with tongues'; not, 'If some speak in the way which I am about to proscribe.' There is a danger that in guarding against the abuse, we may destroy the proper function as well. Paul never intended this to happen. His criticism is ever and always of the abuse. Not a breath was raised against the proper use and he is about to give instruction for this use. Again and again in modern times the wonderful God-glorifying effect of 'tongues' upon the unbeliever has been seen when 'tongues' have been properly used. The word 'unlearned' is even more difficult in this context. It probably simply means those who were not familiar with what was taking place and to whom tongues were quite strange. Presumably 'learned' people would have knowledge of what was transpiring.

But if all prophesy, and there come in one unbelieving or unlearned,[1] he is reproved by all, he is judged by all; the secrets of his heart are made manifest; and so he will fall down on his face and worship God, declaring that God is among you indeed (1 Cor 14:24–25).[2]

Here the generally useful nature of prophecy is emphasised. The use of the word 'all,' however, is most difficult to reconcile with verse 29, in which the prophets are instructed to 'prophesy by two or three'. It almost seems as though the word 'all' is used as an antithesis to the 'all' who speak in tongues in the preceding verse. Here the different reaction is shown and the superior usefulness of prophecy demonstrated. The view that the difficulty may be reconciled by taking the 'two or three' of verse 29 as being the limit for the number prophesying at one and the same time is scarcely tenable, since this would surely lead to disorder and seems against the spirit of verse 27, where tongues are to be interpreted—and that in turn. Verse 31 puts it altogether out of court, for there the prophets are instructed to prophesy 'one by one.' To what then does the limitation of number apply? The whole subject is more fully dealt with in chapter 13.

The difficulty. The reaction of prophecy upon the unbeliever is dwelt upon at length. This has given rise to the feeling of contradiction. It has earlier been stated that prophecy is a sign not to the 'unbeliever' but to the 'believer,' and now its usefulness to the unbeliever is so strongly indicated. There is, however, no contradiction whatever. Although the primary function of prophecy is for the believer, Paul shows how it is incidentally beneficial to the unbeliever, whereas tongues, although initially a sign to the unbeliever, wrongly used, defeat their original purpose altogether and serve neither unbeliever nor believer. Thus Paul's main argument is continued. Tongues uninterpreted, or wrongly used, benefit none, not even the unbeliever to whom they are to be a sign; whereas prophecy, although originally a sign to believers and beneficial to them in a direct way, also benefit the unbeliever. Hence the much greater importance of prophecy than uninterpreted tongues in the church gathering. The difficulty consists in confusing the incidental usefulness of prophecy to the unbeliever, with its being a sign to the believer—two quite different things. The fact that prophecy may apply to the unbeliever does not mean that it is particularly for him or a sign to him rather than to the believer.[3]

Prophecy's positive usefulness to the unbeliever. Similar things to what Paul indicates in this verse are often witnessed today when prophecy is used. The unbeliever is reproved and judged, God's presence is manifestly known and often conviction falls. It is marvellous how one utterance can fit so many varied circumstances in so many individuals at one and the same time. Again and again the inner thoughts are written, as it were, upon the wall, and yet generally in such a way that only the individuals concerned are aware of their full significance. Undue embarrassment is avoided but deep searching takes place.

This concludes Paul's attack upon the abuse.

Notes

[1] 'Unbelieving or unlearned' may be viewed as 'unacquainted with Christianity' or 'unbelieving outsiders.' See Fee, *First Epistle to the Corinthians*, p.685 (notes).

[2] 'God is among you indeed.' Fee observes, 'Along with the great need for local communities to be edified, the reason set forth in this paragraph ought to be sufficient to lead the church to pray for the renewal of the prophetic gift in its ongoing life. It is not simply the presence of prophecy itself that signifies God's presence among his gathered people, but the powerful revealing work of the Spirit that convicts of sin and leads to repen-

tance. Perhaps in our domestication of the Spirit we have also settled for a "safer" expression of worship, one in which very few are ever led to exclaim that "Surely God is among you." Seeing that actually take place leads to prayer that v.1 might be the church's ongoing portion: love, spiritual gifts, especially prophecy.' *Ibid.*, pp.687–88.

3 The Corinthians seem to have thought of tongues as angelic and as a sign of spiritual maturity. Paul here shows that they are a sign not to believers at all but to unbelievers. He is forever anxious to correct the Corinthians on their false views of spirituality.

Various translators have had such difficulty with this passage that they have assumed a textual error has occurred. Fee writes of J. B. Phillips that he, 'without textual warrant, opted for radical surgery and transposed "believer" and "unbeliever" in his translation. He noted: "This is the sole instance of the translator's departing from the accepted text. He felt bound to conclude, from the sense of the next three verses, that we have here either a slip of the pen on the part of Paul, or, more probably, a copyist's error" . . .' *Ibid.*, p.681 (note). The passage, however, is accurate as it stands. Quite simply, Paul, in showing the superiority of prophecy to uninterpreted tongues, indicates that the first, while primarily intended for the believer, suits unbelievers as well, whereas tongues, intended for unbelievers as a sign, wrongly used fail even to meet that end.

13

Positive Instruction for the Use of the Gifts[1]

What is it then, brethren? When ye come together, each one hath a psalm, hath a teaching, hath a revelation, hath a tongue, hath an interpretation. Let all things be done unto edifying (1 Cor 14:26).

The main argument is now concluded and Paul turns to give positive instruction for the church gathering. Members are to be used in the various ministries mentioned and Paul proceeds to show how this is to be done for the general benefit.

Notice that the question mark is after the word 'brethren' (mirroring the pause in the Greek). Some have failed to observe this and have wrongly supposed that Paul is sarcastically asking, 'How is it that you all have these things?' 'Each' would not appear to have all, but rather each one who ministers has one of the following—a psalm, a tongue, etc. Notice the keynote again: 'Let all things be done unto edifying,' The ministries mentioned are straightforward, apart from 'revelation' which is discussed under verse 30.

If any man speaketh in a tongue, let it be by two, or at the most three, and that in turn; and let one interpret (1 Cor 14:27).[2]

Paul now gives his ruling on the use of tongues. Let there be one utterance at a time and let each utterance be interpreted.

'. . . *let one interpret*': The question arises, does 'one' mean someone, the 'one' being impersonal as in the French 'on,' and is Paul merely insisting that the utterances be interpreted; or does 'one' mean the numeral one?

The Greek supports the first view, and this means that Paul allows as many interpreters as there are utterances in one gathering. In present-day practice churches differ—some allow this, while others restrict to one interpreter for all the utterances in one service. I take the first view. Songs also, it should be remembered, are to be interpreted. This in my view, however, would not preclude congregational singing in tongues as already mentioned (p.74).

There is yet another divergence in practice, in the timing of interpretation. In some cases all the utterances in tongues are given before anyone interprets. In others, each interpretation immediately follows the utterance to which it applies. I favour the second practice.

But if there be no interpreter, let him keep silent in the church; and let him speak to himself, and to God (1 Cor 14:28).

This is straightforward but raises a real difficulty which is fully discussed later. How is it possible to make a mistake in the use of the gifts, which should only operate under the Spirit's control? For example, why should Paul require to say in this case, 'let him keep silent'? If the gift is God-unctioned, and since God cannot err, how is any such instruction needed at all? Would it not be quite impossible to give such an utterance when no interpreter was present, since God demanded interpretation? This whole subject is discussed later (see chapter 15).

'. . . *let him speak to himself and to God*': This may be done either in complete silence—speaking in the heart; or, presumably, in an undertone which has no disturbing effect on the assembly. Compare verse 2 where the speaking is to, or before, God.

And let the prophets speak by two or three, and let the others discern (1 Cor 14:29).

The difficulty of the number who may prophesy has been indicated in commenting on verse 24. The matter is again referred to in verse 31, where we read that 'all may prophesy, one by one, that all may learn,' and these verses prevent us from accepting the view that only two or three may prophesy in one service, as appears to be indicated here.

How many then may prophesy? Four possibilities arise:
1. All—'For ye all can prophesy' (v.31).
2. Two or three only—'let the prophets speak by two or three' (v.29).
3. All—but not more than two or three at one time.
4. All—but with one prophet giving not more than two or three utterances.

If verses 24 and 31 alone were to be considered the matter would be perfectly straightforward: for in verse 24 the effect of 'all' prophesying upon the unbeliever is analysed and the practice seems tacitly approved, and in verse 31 it is distinctly stated that all may prophesy. Verse 29, however, alters the position. Here we read, 'And let the prophets speak by two or three.' Thus if 'two or three' refers to prophets taking part the verses are directly contradictory. If a limitation was not being made, there was no point in mentioning number at all. Again, it cannot be maintained that 'all may prophesy,' but no more than two or three in one service—for conduct in one service is the very point under discussion and the church was the place where the 'all' were to prophesy.

To evade the difficulty and reconcile these verses some have suggested a third possibility: namely, that all may prophesy—but no more than two or three at once. No doubt in the early Church many did take part in various exercises at one and the same time, but is it not this very kind of matter which Paul sought to regulate? The Church is to pass from the childhood to the mature state. But verse 31 settles the matter beyond doubt. The prophets are to 'prophesy one by one, that all may learn.' This instruction is in harmony with that relating to tongues, which said that these were to be 'in turn.' Thus this argument fails and with it the view that 'two or three' can possibly refer to the total number of prophets who may take part in one service.

What then can the expression mean? From a study of the Greek alone, a definite ruling cannot be given. The verse is obscure and indeed the governing preposition 'by' is not in the original. It is inserted in italics by the Revisers to make the sentence readable. The original more exactly reads: 'Let the prophets speak two or three and let the others discern.' On the surface the 'two or three' seems to refer to prophets but it might equally mean 'times' or 'prophecies.' In the light of verses 24 and 31, which definitely make the number who may prophesy unlimited, this verse cannot be regarded as placing a limitation on the number who may prophesy. The only solution which seems possible is that the limitation is on the number of prophecies which one individual may give. This may not at first seem attractive, but the difficulty of rejecting it must be faced. With this interpretation all the difficulties are reconciled. All may prophesy but each one who does prophesy must do so in turn and he may not do so more than two or three times in one service.

In actual practice in the present day, conduct has been largely conditioned by verses 24 and 31, no limitation being placed on the number of prophecies. The difficulty of verse 29 has been more or less quietly ignored. Hence, so far as practice is concerned, there is likely to be little change as a result of holding this view. But the immediate corollary of the view could effect change. This has not materialised and yet the conclusion seems inescapable: if the 'two or three' of verse 29 applies to prophetic utterances given by one individual and not to the number of individuals giving these utterances or to the total number of prophecies, then so must the 'two, or at the most three' of verse 27 refer to utterances in tongues by one speaker, not to the number of persons who speak or to the total number of utterances. The two cases are parallel. The same type of construction is used in each; and what is true of one is true of both. This necessitates a closer re-examination of verse 27. We read, 'If any man speaketh in a tongue, let it be by two, or at the most three, and that in turn; and let one interpret.' 'If any man'—singular—'speaketh in a tongue, let it be by two, or at the most three.' Two or three what? Men or tongues? The sense certainly bears the interpretation 'tongues' as well as 'men.' Indeed from the syntax of the sentence this is probably the better rendering. The original may be helpful. It reads more exactly: 'If any man speaketh in a tongue, by two or at the most three, and in turn, and let one interpret.' (The words omitted are in italics in the Revised Version.)

There is one serious objection, however. If the 'two or three' refers to utterances by one individual, to what does the 'in turn' refer? It can scarcely refer to these same utterances, since one individual could not in any case speak in two or three tongues at one time and his utterances would automatically be 'in turn.' From this the 'two or three' would seem more likely to refer to persons, who were not to speak at one and the same time. This would mean that those who spoke in tongues were to do so in turn and no one was to do so more than three times. This is an equally possible rendering of the sense of the passage.

Secondly, the question arises: If the 'two or three' refers to persons, how many utterances may these give? There is just no answer. No legislation is laid down. If we make the 'two or three' a limitation of the persons speaking, we cannot then make it a limitation of their utterances in tongues. If it is a limitation of utterances, then we cannot make it a limitation of persons. Surely the only way out of the difficulty is to view it as a limitation, as in prophecy, on the number of utterances by one individual.

There has been difference in practice amongst Pentecostal people. Three has generally been regarded as the maximum number of utterances in tongues permissible in one service, whether they come from three individuals or from one. But can this be completely justified? To recapitulate, if the 'three' refers to persons, may these not then give an unlimited number of utterances? If it refers to utterances may not an unlimited number of people give them? We can scarcely have it both ways. The 'two or three' cannot be viewed as limiting both speakers and utterances. It seems more reasonable to view the limitation as one upon the number of utterances by one individual.

Thus from a straightforward analysis of the text of verse 27 a very fair case can be made out for more than three utterances in one service. Coupled with the stronger case for more than three utterances in prophecy, the argument is further strengthened. It should be strongly emphasised that the two stand or fall together. The same type of construction is used in each reference and the same arguments are generally applicable.

Now while it has been the general practice in Pentecostal circles to limit the number of utterances in tongues to three while prophecy has been unlimited, it has often been felt that this limitation has had a curbing effect on a large section of the congregation so far as the use of the gift of tongues is concerned. Many have felt unctioned for at least a fourth utterance (which is in itself suggestive) and the above view, which seems to come nearest to solving all the textual difficulties, would meet this difficulty as well.[3]

'. . . *let the others discern*': It is difficult to decide from the phrase itself to whom the word 'others' refers. The Greek gives little help. It might apply to other prophets, or to the rest of the congregation generally. However, if the foregoing view of the number who may prophesy is correct, it would seem that 'others' refers to prophets only. To envisage 'others' referring to the congregation generally raises serious difficulties. How, for example, could those without the gift of prophecy or deep spirituality judge prophetic utterance or how would young immature believers discern such things? The former seems the correct view.

'. . . *discern*': This is a vital word and that in a wide sense. Prophecy must be discerned. It is totally wrong to imagine that everything that purports to be prophecy should be accepted as the voice of God. Too many have erred along this line. It should ever be remembered that there is no cheap, easy, or mechanical way envisaged in Scripture, either of enquiring of the Lord successfully, or of hearing His voice on our own terms. Nor is there any automatic way of giving prophecy. A false or mistaken prophet may give forth of himself but his utterance is to be judged and condemned. Apart from divine unction and illumination the real prophet is powerless. He can neither receive of himself nor give of himself and when he does give, his utterance is to be discerned and will well stand the test. Spiritual things are spiritually discerned and in this way must his prophecy be treated. Mechanical laws cannot easily be laid down for this. It might be said that agreement with Scripture gives an utterance authority. But this simple rule by no means provides for all the difficulties that may arise. While it may be said that if an utterance disagrees with Scripture, it is automatically ruled out, it does not follow that it is always acceptable for a particular place or occasion, merely because it contains no heresy. Something other than an automatic rule is required. How does anyone ever know the voice of God, or the true from the false in spiritual things? Surely the 'wind bloweth where it listeth.' Is it not so in such knowledge? We know not whence it comes. It is spiritual and while things spiritual may be apprehended *through* natural faculties, they are not apprehended merely *by* these. The supra-rational and supernatural are involved and these forever escape rational or natural definition. Hence Paul's later appeal: 'If any man thinketh himself to be a prophet, or spiritual, let him take knowledge of the things which I write unto you, that they are the commandment of the Lord.' (Note—not, 'If any man is learned or brilliant'!) In other words, his appeal is to the spiritual faculty. By this, prophecy is to be judged. In practice, it is not generally difficult to tell whether prophecy is under unction, or otherwise; and whether it is of God or a manifestation of the natural masquerading in spiritual realms. When false prophecy is given, true prophets and spiritual people in a congregation are likely to find a clear knowledge on their spirits of the error. The matter is not nearly so obscure and difficult in practice as it might seem from an intellectual scanning of the chapter. In such discerning, of course, the tremendous and impassable barrier between flesh and spirit, natural mind and spiritual mind, becomes apparent. The two conditions and the two outlooks are worlds apart. Also the importance of spiritual endowment in the oversight of an assembly becomes evident when such things require to be dealt with in normal church life.[4]

Finally, it should be remembered that there may be as much danger in rejecting a true message from God, as in accepting a mistaken utterance.

Notes

[1] The greater part of this chapter appears as Appendix 3 in the author's *Reflections on the Gifts of the Spirit*.

[2] As Fee remarks: 'What is said here about tongues is precisely in keeping with what Paul has argued throughout; it serves as further evidence that he has not been after tongues as such, but after uninterpreted tongues in the assembly. Here he regulates the use of tongues *with* interpretation' (*First Epistle to the Corinthians*, pp.689–690).

[3] Fee writes: 'First, "two—or at the most three—should speak." One cannot be sure whether this means "at any one service" or "before there is an interpretation." In favor of the former is the phrase "at the most," plus the overall concern of the chapter that tongues not dominate the assembly; therefore in this guideline Paul is suggesting that such manifestations be limited in any given meeting. In favor of the latter is the similar recommendation for prophecies in vv.29–31, which on the basis of vv.24 and 31 is intended to limit the number of speakers in sequence, not the number of prophecies at any given service. On the whole, this is not easy to decide, but probably the word "at the most," which is missing in the guidelines for prophecies, tips the balance in favor of the former' (*First Epistle to the Corinthians*, p.691).

Prior to reading this it had never occurred to me (nor, I imagine, to most of the Pentecostal world) that anything other than limitation for a total service was under consideration in Paul's instructions— but if Fee's suggestion that the limitation was simply that only two or three were to speak in tongues before there was interpretation is correct, it alters the whole picture. It removes limitation on total numbers of both people speaking and utterances given in tongues in a total service. Similarly the limitation regarding prophecy would simply be to the number who may speak in sequence, and not to the total number who might take part in a whole service.

My own writing has been based on the assumption that conduct over a whole service was envisaged—but I find this insight of Dr. Fee very persuasive, and while he himself is not wholly convinced on the tongues limitation, his argument has affected my thinking. I have, however, let my writing stand. It was on this that Appendix 3 in Reflections on the Gifts of the Spirit *was based, and if conduct in a total service is envisaged it remains relevant. To be honest, however, I now believe the view suggested by Fee is correct.*

Let me recapitulate and clarify. The relevant verses impose some kind of limitation, and the most likely limitation is on persons rather than utterances—but to avoid the seeming contradiction between prophets prophesying by two or three and all prophesying, the suggestion was made that utterances rather than persons may have been intended. I have always felt, however, that this is strained. For me the whole difficulty now disappears by viewing Paul's instructions as applying to phases in a service rather than to the whole service. The limitation, I now definitely feel, is on persons and not utterances.

4 The question arises about the practical outworking of the discernment of prophecy. I am not persuaded that there was a formal process with a time set apart for this with a delivered judgment. Rather I see it as something happening spontaneously and intervention only taking place if something wrong was given. In practice, I find it necessary to deal with this publicly on very few occasions. If something heretical or obviously unanointed is given, it should be dealt with. If minor error has slipped in, help can be given privately.

14

Positive Instructions Concluded

But if a revelation be made to another sitting by, let the first keep silence (1 Cor 14:30).

The discussion of revelation has been postponed until this point. The word is translated from *apokaluptō* meaning to uncover or disclose (noun: *apokalupsis*). The question arises: Is revelation a type of prophecy or is it something quite different?

The argument against revelation as a type of prophecy is simply that in verse 6 Paul speaks of revelation, knowledge, prophesying, doctrine. The fact that both revelation and prophecy appear in the same list seems to argue in favour of a distinction in meaning.

The counter-argument is that in verse 26 the word 'prophecy' is omitted and 'revelation' is included. Remembering the importance that Paul attached to prophecy this seems extremely strange unless provision is made for its inclusion under a different name. That this is indeed so, seems apparent when the meaning of 'revelation' is compared with the function of prophecy. A revelation is an uncovering, a manifestation, a disclosure. Is this not exactly in accord with what is pictured as happening when an unbeliever hears prophecy (vv.24–25)?

In addition, the fact that both words are in verse 6 does not mean that the two are different. It may well be that prophecy includes revelation, although revelation may not necessarily include all aspects of prophecy.

Surely every revelation is prophetic in a sense that need have nothing to do with vocal utterance. It is difficult to conceive of any God-given, God-unctioned revelation being given to the Church about anything which could not be termed prophetic in that sense. But the type of revelation mentioned in verse 30 is for utterance and the utterance is not private but public and would necessarily be God-unctioned and hence prophetic in nature.[1]

A further study of the present verse lends even more support to the view. There is no reason to think that the two words are not here used quite synonymously. Paul is further underlining the instruction that utterances in prophecy are to be given by course. The first prophet is to be silent, while the second gives his message. This is merely another way of saying that both are not to speak at once. There is not necessarily any thought in the text of the second interrupting the first. Two questions however arise. How is the first to know to be silent unless he is interrupted? And why did Paul not rather instruct the second to keep silent until the first had finished?

It must be remembered that Paul is here dealing with abuses of spiritual gifts. It is possible for individuals to speak in tongues, for instance, without real unction and mistakenly. It is also possible for them to continue speaking as though in prophecy after the real unction for utterance has passed. This is not to be. Such a one is to be silent and give place to another who has received a genuine revelation. On the surface Paul may not appear here to be referring to an abuse of prophecy but merely to be regulating its use; but how else can such conduct as is implied be regarded? It has sometimes been suggested that particular light or revelation may be given on some point arising in prophecy which might give rise to an interruption and that it is this particular revelation, as distinct from prophecy generally, to which Paul refers. But unless there was very keen sensitivity to the Spirit would this not tend to lead to just the kind of confusion which the apostle is seeking to avoid? Is the prophetic utterance to be held in abeyance while revelation is given on a particular point and then to continue later? It may be so, but the real meaning seems to be simpler and more straightforward. Indeed its very simplicity may have given rise to the difficulty of apprehension—a revelation may well be neither more nor less than the illumination and utterance which a prophet often receives and gives, and although the injunction to be silent is given to the first rather than the second speaker this may be no more than a different way of saying that only one is to speak at a time.

For ye all can prophesy one by one, that all may learn, and all may be comforted (1 Cor 14:31).

This is already largely dealt with. Notice the word 'comforted.' This may also be read 'exhorted.' Some have put an over-emphasis on the 'comfort' element in prophecy. God generally comforts those in need or deserving (and indeed undeserving!), but often before comfort can be administered there must be sharp rebuke. Rebuke may of course be included in 'prophecy' under the heading 'edification' (v.3). Men are often broken down before they are built up and even backslidden believers may find that prophecy affects them as it did the unbelievers of verse 25—being reproved and judged. This function of prophecy must not be overlooked.

And the spirits of the prophets are subject to the prophets (1 Cor 14:32).

This is a vital verse, containing a principle that runs far beyond the immediate context of the verse. 'The spirits of the prophets are subject to the prophets.' Now God, so far as the present writer is aware, never turns people into automatic creatures, functioning under His power, with their own wills rendered powerless. Even in the Baptism in the Spirit, it would be possible, though deeply grieving to God, for the individual baptized to rise and leave the place of baptism, more or less at will. In actuality man becomes more controlled, not less, under the afflatus of the Spirit. God always integrates personality. That which disintegrates is never of Himself. Hysteria, ill-temper and all other things causing loss of control in this way, can never be attributed to God. In the Baptism and in deep anointings for use in the gifts, the individual has the feeling of never being more alive, balanced and controlled. He is conscious of divine presence and guidance but in submitting to this he is also conscious of the enhancement of his natural endowments. Perfect submission has produced perfect freedom. Licence brought bondage and crippling; now bond-service has brought liberty and release. There is an impression of being a whole man, an integrated being—functioning at the highest reach of his powers—with the impression of those powers not so much functioning as being functioned through—not initiating action, but enjoying full-blooded action at the highest.

This of course pays little court to the view that the mind is and should be supreme in man.[2] In personal experience, I have never known greater perfection or beauty of language than that heard in the gifts of the Spirit; and in my own case, I have never known greater intellectual power and perception than when the mind is denied the primary place and the Spirit allowed to control. The mind, in the secondary role, becomes hypersensitive and keen. One has the impression of at last fulfilling a role and function for which one has been born. So to act is to become alive. So far as natural action and thinking are concerned, there is a passivity, but the passivity is not that of death but of boundless life—and the activity in that state far surpasses the activity of the natural condition, in which the mind is dominant.[3] Instead of the woolly thinking, the faltering concentration, the distracting influence of pirate thoughts, there is full, clear concentration and the creation of utterances and concepts of beauty and truth which are completely satisfying and edifying to one's own soul and to the souls of the hearers.

It should be underlined again for those who would dismiss the spiritual gifts as ecstatic utterances, associated with a primitive state in the life of the Church, that men like Paul were intellectual giants by any standard and in any age. And yet such a man as he so strongly exhorts his hearers to seek such gifts and he himself values them so highly. He realised that his education, his intellectual brilliance, were as nothing compared to the unction and illumination of the Spirit. Many a time the present writer has thanked God that he has had the benefit of higher education, that he might know its limits as well as its scope. The mind becomes so much keener in the use of the gifts of the Spirit than in any merely natural function. The gifts 'rudimentary and primitive?' Rather the reverse— 'illumined and mature!'

There is a strange fallacy popular in some circles that the church of Corinth was a carnal unspiritual church, far behind the churches of many of our large denominations today. We regard ourselves as cultured now, educated, mature. One moment! In those days miracles were performed in the Name of Christ, the sick were healed, the heathen were converted, the demon-possessed were delivered. In short, the works of Christ were wrought. Were churches in which, and through which, such things took place inferior to what, in our day, have often become declining social institutions? Do the lame now walk, do the wicked turn to righteousness? Too often, not only have the ecstatic utterances ceased, but the life of Christ itself has largely, if not quite, departed, and Christianity has been largely replaced by pseudo-morality and social custom. The fact that church members may on the whole be better educated than the early believers does not mean that they are better Christians—or for that matter Christians at all.[4] Breadth or depth of learning is no substitute for holiness and indeed is in itself quite useless in the things of God. It is not, unless under divine control, necessarily a weapon or a glory in the Kingdom at all. Holiness not culture, goodness not cleverness, are the hallmarks. If in God's eyes Corinth was carnal, and, to a degree, carnal she was, may God help us! When Paul wrote, Corinth had but recently been converted from heathenism and when sin entered, it could be horrible sin, not to be tolerated either then or now. But as well as lack of experience, immaturity, division and in one case gross immorality, she had in her midst the priceless possession of the real power of the Spirit of God.

It is my sober and considered conviction that Corinth, although carnal in various ways and seriously lacking in love, was in other ways both mature and advanced in comparison with many churches in our age. The supercilious, superior attitude which contemptuously looks from modern heights upon carnal Corinth is lamentably mistaken.

To revert to the text ('the spirits of the prophets are subject to the prophets') we may conclude that lack of control may never be attributed to God. The prophet is always responsible—and the stronger the unction the greater the control. The principle holds even to the deepest depth of unconsciousness in God. To such a place one goes out completely controlled. Human faculties in such a state may be transcended but, although transcended, they are in safe hands—the hands of God. For people to lose control, in the normal sense of that word, is to cause the unction to tend to depart and the Spirit to be grieved. People with little control in the natural, tend to be unable to bear heavy unction in the spiritual. Indiscipline in the one sphere is reflected in the other. Hence undisciplined people are comparatively useless to God—and this principle applies in many fields.

For God is not a God of confusion, but of peace; as in all the churches of the saints (1 Cor 14:33).[5]

Who causes the confusion? Evidently those who abuse the gifts. Those who lose control and blame God. Notice that to lose control is quite a different thing from becoming God-abandoned. The two have too often been confused. We are responsible to be the one. The other we must shun like the plague. The only losing of control that we may allow is the losing of it in God; in which case, paradoxically enough, we retain it ten-fold. Some may ask, but how can control be lost in the things of the Spirit? It is very easy for a person with impure or mistaken motives[6] to be in a spiritual state in a gathering where the presence of God is powerful and to allow natural faculties to come into play and masquerade in a spiritual guise. It is similar, in a sense, to turning the grace of God into lasciviousness in another realm. The power is true and real, but it is wasted by faulty instruments seeking to divert it into mistaken channels. Thus a person may be unctioned to intercede powerfully in private, but prefer to be seen of men, and rise and endeavour to turn the power as it were to public prayer. The unction may depart, but he may try to imitate in his prayer the effect of it. Some may scream and shout in a hysterical and wrong way when the presence of God falls, to the grieving of the Spirit. In such cases there should be control, and utterances and actions, though impassioned, will be beautiful and edifying—God Himself controlling His servants.

Notes

1. According to Fee, 'Paul uses the word "revelation" in a variety of ways, but only in the present argument to suggest some kind of utterance given by the Spirit for the benefit of the gathered community. Precisely what its content might be and how it would differ from "knowledge" or "prophecy" is not at all clear. For example, along with "teaching" it appears in the final list in v.26 . . . Perhaps in the final list (v.26) this word covers both prophecy and knowledge as the more inclusive term. In any case, it implies the disclosure of divine "mysteries," either about the nature of the gospel itself (cf. 2:10) or perhaps about things otherwise hidden to the "natural man" ' (*First Epistle to the Corinthians*, pp.662–63).

2. See Appendix 1.

3. The question of passivity is further explored in Appendix 5. Also of interest is the following question: Is there any relation between a particular individual's human personality and the gifts of the Spirit which operate in him? In other words, does a person who receives interpretation or prophecy, for instance, generally have good natural powers of expression? To my mind, the answer is in the affirmative, although not all Pentecostal teachers would agree. It does seem that while the gifts are by no means natural, they function through natural faculties, and while we may all potentially have in varying measure all the faculties necessary for the functioning of all the gifts, these are not given to all—and it may be that they are given to those through whom they can be best used. The gift of prophecy, for example, may be more evident in certain types of people than in others. The gift of healing may be more prominent in certain families than in others. The names of George, Stephen and Edward Jeffreys immediately spring to mind in this connection. To say these things in no way detracts from the divine origin and functioning of the gifts.

4. In a favourite quotation from C. S. Lewis, 'If you send a devil to Oxford you merely make him a clever devil.'

5. According to Fee, 'The concluding word on prophecies (vv.32–33) probably functions as a concluding word for the whole section' (*First Epistle to the Corinthians*, p.688). Fee further comments, 'Paul is arguing that the basis of all these

instructions is ultimately theological. It has to do with the character of God, probably vis-à-vis the deities of the cults, whose worship was characterized by frenzy and disorder. The theological point is crucial: the character of one's deity is reflected in the character of one's worship . . . God is neither characterized by disorder nor the cause of it in the assembly' (*ibid.*, p.697). On the last phrase ('so in all the churches of the saints'), Fee writes: 'Because of some apparent awkwardness in speaking of God in this way, the NIV follows a number of scholars who prefer to take this final phrase with vv.34–35. But there are a number of reasons for taking it as the concluding word to these instructions on "order." (a) As will be noted in the next section, there is substantial evidence that vv.34–35 are not authentic, and therefore that Paul could not have intended it to go with what he did not write. In any case, the very early textual evidence in the Western church indicates that this phrase was not considered to be part of vv.34–35. (b) The two rhetorical questions in v.36, both of which begin with "or," make best sense when understood as referring directly to this statement. That is, "All the churches of the saints are intended to be orderly as we have just described, *or* did the word of God originate with you?" This seems to be the proper understanding of the rhetoric of v.36, even if vv.34–35 are authentic . . . .

'Thus, this final appeal continues the theological word with which the sentence began. God is not only like this, but he has so ordered that his character be appropriately displayed in worship in all the churches. This particular appeal, which in this letter began with the opening words of salutation (see 1:2), is an indication to the Corinthians that their view of tongues and spirituality that has allowed this kind of disorderly conduct is out of keeping with what God is doing elsewhere through the gospel. They are marching to their own drum; Paul is urging them not only to conform to the character of God, but also to get in step with the rest of his church' (*ibid.*, pp.697–98).

Fee adds, 'But it is no great credit to the historical church that in opting for "order" it also opted for a silencing of the ministry of the many. That, it would seem, is at least the minimal point of the paragraph.

'The most important word in this paragraph is the final one.

Some Pentecostal and charismatic assemblies would do well to heed these directives; confusion and disorder is simply not in keeping with the character of God. On the other hand, v.26 makes it clear that the "peace" and "order" of v.33 do not necessarily mean somber ritual . . . If our understanding of God's character is revealed in our worship, then it must be admitted that God is not often thought of in terms of allowing spontaneity or of joy' (*ibid.*, p.698).

6 In case confusion of thought arises, it should be explained that God unctions clean vessels, but it is possible for human frailty to manifest itself, even after unction falls—and for mistaken and wrong motives to creep in. This can cause abuses in the gifts.

15

Conclusion of the Matter

Verses 34–36 are dealt with in *A Trumpet Call to Women* and may be bypassed here. Suffice to say that I disagree with Hurley's suggestion that the 'silence' of women referred to the discerning of prophecy. I note that Fee, although a conservative scholar, is of the view that the verses were not in the original Scripture.[1]

> *If any man thinketh himself to be a prophet, or spiritual, let him take knowledge of the things which I write unto you, that they are the commandment of the Lord* (1 Cor 14:37).

This has been largely discussed, but again one of the problems postponed earlier raises its head and may conveniently be dealt with at this point. Here Paul speaks of the instructions which he has given. Now the fact of these instructions raises a fundamental problem. The person coming initially to this chapter finds it most difficult to understand how there can be any possible error in the use of gifts of the Spirit. 'Surely,' he argues, 'these function only under divine power—and if so, error, or the need for instruction in use, cannot possibly arise.' Such is just not the case! Ideally it is what God intends, but in practice it is not always achieved. The unctioning power is perfect but the material unctioned is fallible.

There are two ways in which error commonly arises. There may be unprincipled people who endeavour to imitate a gift. For example, a person may speak as though in prophecy without any unction whatever. This is very easily discerned and needs no comment.

Some may be more genuinely mistaken. They may find themselves in a pregnant atmosphere. They become aware of the moving of the Spirit upon them—and, without continuing to wait for the clear direction and full unction of God, immediately burst into utterance. It is, as has already been indicated, the entrance of the natural into spiritual realms. Instead of divine power flowing through the intended channel, an attempt (albeit unintentional) is made to divert it, with devastating and frustrating consequences.

Thus 'tongues' may be heard, seemingly in a message, when unction was given for private intercession. Such may go uninterpreted—not because there is no interpreter present, but because of the initial error. The question immediately arises in many minds: 'Can a person then speak in tongues, or in what seems like tongues, in a mistaken way, or even quite without unction?' The answer is definitely, 'Yes!' When that gift is once given, the recipient is generally able ever after, to speak in 'tongues' or in what seems like 'tongues' at will.

It is my opinion that what is then spoken, at least in the latter case, is mere imitation and senseless—but the point is, it can be done and can lead to real confusion. Under real unction all is sweet and harmonious. Otherwise disorder ensues. These facts clearly emerge, not only from the text of this chapter, but from general practice. While the gifts are in themselves perfect and God-given, they ought also to be, and only to be, fully God-unctioned and God-controlled in operation.

Is error inevitable? Not at all! Perfection is possible and ought always to be achieved. Man is no less responsible for error in this than in other realms.

There is, however, overshadowing this, a still deeper problem. Did Paul conceive of a person being unctioned to act in a way contrary to his regulations and, in such a case, more or less say, 'The spirit of the prophet is subject to the prophet, so obey my injunction?' If so, it would be to admit of two authorities and lead to ultimate contradiction. We must accept it as a fundamental principle that God is never divided and never unctions anyone to do what would amount to disobedience to His own commandment. Nor did Paul think so. He does not make his instructions the basis or mainspring of action in the use of gifts. His regulations, he said, were the 'commandment of God.' In short he might say, 'If you are really unctioned and you carefully obey your unction, you will act along those lines and you will do this not principally because I make the regulation but because this is the way God Himself leads.'

Paul is to be conceived as not so much giving a commandment as interpreting a position, and these are very different things. He never conceived of people choosing between two authorities—his commandment and the activity of the Spirit. He never regarded obedience to the latter leading to conflict with the former. Paul appealed to the prophets and spiritual people, as those who would know, supernaturally know, that the instructions he gave were of God. To argue that the two authorities clash is to open the door to the denial of the inspiration of Paul's epistle.

These points may seem belaboured—but they are of tremendous importance. Through misunderstanding them, some have tended to downgrade the gifts to more or less natural functions of the human spirit—in which error is quite to be expected and is scarcely more culpable than in normal preaching. The reverse is true. Paul demanded perfection. His assault was always on what resulted from lack of abandonment to God in the use of the gifts. He shows how things will function if His unction is obeyed. Now a mere mechanical obedience to the detail of the regulations, as for example in number of utterances, does not in itself give perfection. Basic to all is the voice of the Spirit. When this is fully obeyed, regulations are super-fluous in that they are fully fulfilled; and in all that is given, there is life and truth and harmony. Error alone causes the abuses. The wrong practices were never of the Spirit.

'. . . *let him take knowledge*': Paul is not merely asking that his readers accept his teachings as the commandment of the Lord because Paul says so. He appeals to their own claim to be 'prophet(s), or spiritual,' implying that if truly spiritual they will themselves recognise (*epiginōskō*) the truth of his statement.

> But if any man is ignorant, let him be ignorant (1 Cor 14:38).[2]

The authoritative note sounds here and properly so. Notice how often this sounds in Paul's writings. The man of God must always have authority. Paul brooks no argu-ment. 'Thus saith the Lord.' The Church never was, nor was it ever intended to be, democratic. The people are not consulted on matters of church government and doctrine. The rule is theocratic—coming through a narrow chan-nel—from the apostles downwards. The rule always comes through the few, spiritually endowed, to the many. The 'many' are not consulted—they are commanded. It is ever so in spiritual things. Frequently a movement of God may be traced back to the word of God to one individual. Such a one does not consult or argue. He receives com-mands and he gives commands—and if any is ignorant, he is ignorant to his own confusion. Let him remain so! All is said! Such a view may not be popular but it is so obviously correct. When the Apostle went to a heathen community he spoke as with the voice of God. The word was in demonstration of the Spirit and with power. There was no appeal nor could there be to an authoritative book such as the Bible—the Scriptures which did exist carried no weight with such audiences—hence there could be no argument about interpretation. There came crashing into the world of the hearer the voice of God. It was accepted or rejected. If rejected it was rejected against light—the individual knowing he had met God and turned aside. The appeal is to the spiritual faculty within—to the part by which men know right from wrong. After their conversion Paul continues to deal with people in the same way. The voice is always authoritative. Sometimes the authority is delegated as, for example, to Timothy, or to appointed elders. In no case are the people generally invited to share the spiritual rule.

These views may, of course, wrongly interpreted, lead to an evil worse even than democracy within the Church; namely, non-Spirit-led autocracy, either through an individual or a group. Unless the Spirit is in control no system functions properly. When He is in control, He may use many diverse systems, although the one described above seems to be nearest to the New Testament pattern. It is one which gives God great control. 'Few' seem easier to control and direct, than 'many.' Hence the vesting of power in their hands. On the other hand, there is an element of safety with the 'many.'

Wherefore, my brethren, desire earnestly to prophesy, and forbid not to speak with tongues (1 Cor 14:39).

This verse effectively summarises the whole. The first injunction is accepted generally, although often by misin terpreting the word 'prophesy' and calling it 'preaching.' The second injunction is too often overlooked by many. Let it be underlined. Paul said it: '. . . *forbid not to speak with tongues.*' In view of the confusion in Corinth, some were possibly so doing. In another case he had to instruct, 'Despise not prophesying,' probably again because abuse had brought the ministry into disrepute. The criticism must ever and only be applied to the abuse—never to the God-glorifying, man-edifying use. Paul said it. Who has countermanded the order? When did the practice cease? History tells us plainly—'Never!'[3] We read of it in the following centuries: second, fourth, twelfth to fifteenth, seventeenth, eighteenth, nineteenth, twentieth. In our own day it is increasingly common. Millions now possess the gift. As never before, the Spirit is being out-poured upon all flesh. Surely the fulfilment of Joel's prediction is taking place as we approach the end time.[4] Praise God!

The revival of the gifts in the Church led to the formation of the Pentecostal movement in the earlier part of the century and more recently to the Charismatic movement. Millions of people have been affected. Powerful gifts of the Spirit are in regular use. The miraculous is in evidence. In a materialistic age, the supernatural power of God has been abundantly demonstrated. Not only this, but in the years following the writing of the original manuscript for this book, other supernatural or occult powers have risen to prominence in our culture. These cannot be effectively combated by a Church that has forgotten to tarry for the 'power from on high.' A return to New Testament foundations has been found the answer, and I believe the only answer, to the spiritual delusions and occult practices of our modern age, as well as its agnosticism and materialism.

But let all things be done decently and in order (1 Cor 14:40).[5]

'. . . *decently and in order*': Yes, indeed! But the decency and order are not sophistication and dryness, nor are they the decency and the order which characterise the grave-yard. There can be holy joy and the expression of it; heart-felt praise and the rapture of it; mouths filled with laughter and the sweetness of it. Lips may sing, and that with fervency, and this commandment still remain uninfringed. 'Rejoice, and again I say unto you rejoice,' wrote this same writer. 'O clap your hands, all ye peoples; shout unto God with the voice of triumph,' wrote the psalmist. Let there be order! Yes, indeed! But let it be the 'order' of the Father's House. Let it be the 'order' of Heaven.

The last of the psalms forms an appropriate commentary and conclusion:

> *Praise ye the Lord.*
> *Praise God in His sanctuary:*
> *Praise Him in the firmament of His power.*
> *Praise Him for His mighty acts:*
> *Praise Him according to His excellent greatness.*
> *Praise Him with the sound of the trumpet:*
> *Praise Him with the psaltery and harp.*
> *Praise Him with the timbrel and dance:*
> *Praise Him with stringed instruments and the pipe.*
> *Praise Him upon the loud cymbals:*
> *Praise Him upon the high-sounding cymbals.*
> *Let everything that hath breath praise the Lord.*

Notes

[1] 'Although these two verses are found in all known manuscripts, either here or at the end of the chapter, the two text-critical criteria of transcriptional and intrinsic probability combine to cast considerable doubt on their authenticity' (Fee, *First Epistle to the Corinthians*, p.699).

[2] Fee comments: 'With the authority of the same Lord from whom he received the "command," Paul pronounces sentence on those who do not recognize the Spirit in what he writes: "If

anyone (i.e., the one who thinks he is a Spirit person) ignores this, he himself will be ignored."

'Paul's point is clear; the precise meaning of the repeated verb is slightly less so. He seems to be making a double play on words. The verb "to ignore" is here the antonym of "acknowledge" in v.37. Thus, a spiritual person should "recognize" what Paul writes as "from the Lord"; if anyone "fails to acknowledge" it as such, that person will in turn not be "recognized/acknowledged." Although it is possible that Paul meant the subject of this last clause to be himself or the church (= "not recognized to be a prophet or spiritual"), more likely "God" is intended. That is, failure to recognize the Spirit in Paul's letter will lead to that person's failure to be "recognized" by God (cf. 8:2–3). Hence it is a prophetic sentence of judgment on those who fail to heed this letter' (*ibid.*, p.712).

³ See Appendix 3.

⁴ See Appendix 6.

⁵ This finishes the chapter. 'But,' as Fee notes, 'the letter itself is not finished. Lying behind their view of spirituality is not simply a false view of spiritual gifts, but a false theology of spiritual existence as such. Since their view of "spirituality" had also brought them to deny a future resurrection of the body, it is fitting that this matter be taken up next'—which it is in chapter 15. Fee adds: 'It is of some interest that people who believe so strongly in the Bible as the Word of God should at the same time spend so much energy getting around the plain sense of vv.39–40. Surely there is irony in that. What Paul writes in these chapters he claims to be the command of the Lord; one wonders how he might have applied v.38 to those who completely reject this command.' (Fee, *First Epistle to the Corinthians*, p.713).

PART 2:

GLIMPSES OF REVIVAL
(With the Testimony of Mary MacLean)

16

Relationship between Pentecost and Revival

When the manuscript from which this book has developed was first written, Pentecostal doctrine suffered a form of attack which is less common now than it was then. It was suggested that Christ and the Cross became less central in the experience of the believers who became Pentecostal and that they became slightly 'off-beam.' Historic revival was accepted as being of God and was to be diligently sought. This 'new' thing was viewed with suspicion and indeed in many cases was viciously opposed.

From my early days as a Christian I had been interested in revival and I had been deeply affected by Finney's description of his own Baptism in the Spirit. In his life and experience there was strong evidence of revival and Baptism being linked—although at that time I had not been particularly conscious of this.

As the years passed I read almost all I could find on revival and in due time was baptized in the Holy Spirit.[1] I found myself in the midst of controversy on tongues and heard the accusation that Pentecost detracted from the Cross and the centrality of Christ. I did not believe it. It was not true of my own experience or of the experience of those who were most deeply in Pentecost. Indeed I had seen in such people a quality of life and devotion to Christ of which I had had no previous knowledge. With me it was like what the late Rev. Duncan Campbell said when he met the two old praying ladies of Barvas who had been behind his invitation to Lewis. (I paraphrase) 'I found that these women had a relationship with God which I did not know existed. They knew Him as I did not know Him. To them he was a covenant keeping God and their intimacy was so great that they would use language like this with all reverence: "Lord, you have promised to send revival. If you do not, how shall we ever be able to trust your word again?" Their faith was absolute. They laid hold on the promises of God and received the things for which they prevailed.'

I discovered a depth of love for Christ and an intimacy at the heart of Pentecost of which I had never previously even dreamed. As it happened, there had been historic revival in Lewis in 1939 and about ten years later with Mr. Campbell, and it became possible for me to observe the relationship between Pentecost as I knew it and revival as the Church generally regarded it.

The basic question was: were they two separate and divergent matters—or were they really one?

I can categorically state that the Spirit of revival is the Spirit of Pentecost and the Spirit of Pentecost is the Spirit of revival—but having said that, I must add that there can be revival without certain Pentecostal manifestations and there can be Pentecostal manifestations without revival— although when both come to their fullest development I would expect them to be one. Pentecost flows from revival and can lead to it.

I found myself on Lewis, at the call of God and in the aftermath of revival. I observed situations and people very closely. I found that converts of the revival were very open and hungry for the outpouring of the Spirit and many received powerfully when they realised that this experience was for them. They gladly entered in—but I also found that without any preaching or teaching about Pentecost, people had been baptized in the Spirit during revival. I cited one case in *Reflections on the Baptism in the Holy Spirit*. A young man of Garrabost was wonderfully saved from long bondage (and known bondage) in sin. He had a vision of Christ and was spoken to by Christ on the open road when others were present. Within twenty-four hours he was baptized in the Spirit, speaking in tongues of which he had had no previous knowledge and which he did not understand. This man became a man of prayer. I have known spiritual darkness recede as he made intercession.

In the village of Balintrushal, near Shader, Barvas, I came on a second case, and the story of the lady concerned forms the second part of this book.

God had spoken to me quite clearly and commissioned me to carry Pentecost to Lewis (see the account of this in *Reflections on the Gifts of the Spirit*). In the course of doing so I arrived one day in Balintrushal and on the advice of a friend called on a Mrs. Mary MacLean. I had not intimated my coming by phone (there was none), letter or messenger—but that did not mean that she did not know of my arrival—oh no! God spoke to her in the morning and told her about me and how she was to treat me! This was not unusual with Mary. She lived this way and God very frequently spoke to her. I very much appreciated what He said to her about me and things between us got off to an excellent start. First, while I knew that God had sent me to people generally with a very definite message, I also felt that there were old saints in Lewis who had experienced powerful revival and who knew God in depth and in ways which might be quite unknown to me and I was very willing, indeed anxious, to sit at their feet and learn. So, basically, I wanted both to impart and receive.

We talked a bit and turned to prayer. I laid hands on Mary and suddenly she began to speak in tongues and when we rose from our knees she looked at me and said, 'That is what happened to me in '39 but I never knew what it was.' She unfolded to me some of her experiences during that revival and I quickly realised that I was in the presence of a saint of God. She had been out of the body in vision for most of a fortnight, seeing the dead of her own area going into Heaven and hell. She had seen the progress of the war—with the fall of France coming before eventual victory. She knew of the defeat of Germany. The secrets of the Lord were with one who feared him. She saw Christ Himself.

I found tremendous spiritual affinity with this old lady (now 83) and she became one of my closest friends—a faithful, loyal but sometimes disconcerting friend. She upheld and indeed still upholds me constantly in prayer but not only does she pray—she also knows of times of difficulty or trouble and I have known me get a message, 'What were you doing at such and such a time? I was much burdened for you.' It could be the very hour that I was in battle with darkness. It is better to have one person like this on your side than ten thousand passengers—where conflict with hell is concerned. I have always felt it one of the signal privileges of my life to have had this lady's friendship. But before I go on to tell her story, I would like to speak a little about the two most recent revivals in Lewis and in particular the 1939 revival.

Notes

[1] See my *Reflections on the Baptism in the Holy Spirit*.

17

Revivals in Lewis

First Meeting the Gobha

In so far as I have been able to trace it, there is no long tradition of revival in Lewis. Prior to 1939 I have no knowledge of any major movement after the first coming of the gospel to the Island except that of 1818–1829.

As a result of this I imagine that the outbreak of the 1939 revival must have had a profound effect on those who experienced it and particularly on those who were God's instruments in its coming. From experiences I have heard from those in this category I gained the impression that they did not at first fully know what was happening to them—they did not have the experiences of an older generation to refer to. They were entering a new and comparatively unknown dimension. It must have taken tremendous spiritual courage and trust to go through with God. They were true pioneers of the spiritual way.

Little is generally known about the '39 revival partly because war came in that year and probably had some effect in diverting attention from it, and partly because very little seems to have been written about it. It was of comparatively short duration, but it was of exceptional power. Again and again I have heard it said that it was a much more powerful revival than the one which followed about ten years later. I have wondered if, in fact, the second was in some ways an outflow from the first; certainly many of the people involved in the second had been involved in the first. The second, however, is much more widely known. It came after the end of the war and attracted the attention of the Christian world beyond Lewis. It has also been described in various publications.

I have not conducted a full and accurate historical enquiry into the subject, but from people who were in the '39 revival I have learned a number of interesting but sometimes isolated facts. Spiritual fire was evidently seen above a church in Lochs at the beginning of events and the man who saw it indicated that revival was coming. It did come. Lochs was deeply affected and people went from there to Point and it broke out powerfully there as it did later in Barvas.

My first knowledge of this movement came very close to the event. The late Rev. John McLeod, once minister of the Free Church, Greenock, was himself a Lewis man and had, I think, gone north and been present when the fire was burning. He spoke to me of the power of God sweeping a congregation and perhaps half of the company going out into a spiritual dimension as their bodies became rigid. It was a trance-like condition (and don't be critical of trances—there are good trances as well as bad ones. Remember Peter and his condition when he saw the sheet with the animals in vision. Similarly don't be critical of Christian people who manifest phenomenal powers simply because strange phenomena also occur in the realm of the occult. Thank God that Moses withstood Janes and Jambres the Egyptian wizards. Thank God that men of God have proved stronger than witch doctors in the recent Indonesian Revival. We should manifest greater power than Satan's emissaries ever wield. Do not be afraid of the trance when it means going out into unconsciousness in God—which is, in fact, to experience a greater consciousness).

From two people who were deeply involved in the '39 revival (intimate acquaintances of Mrs MacLean, as it happens) I learned a number of things at first hand. They are both dead now and had I realised in earlier days that I would be writing this book I might have probed at even greater depth than I did then.

The first was a blacksmith in Shader generally known as the 'Gobha' (pronounced 'go'). I had heard a good deal about him before I first met him. He was very well-known on the Island and was an excellent precentor (leader of song). He was also known as a man of prayer and a responsible, godly man. I gathered, however, that he was not favourably disposed to Pentecost and I suspect that he had been influenced by the view that Pentecost diverted attention from Christ and the Cross. He was not present at the first meetings I held in his area (intentionally, I imagine), but his great friend Roddy Alick had been there and had been very favourably impressed. I remember after the first meeting Roddy had exclaimed, 'Well, I thank God I came here and have seen and heard for myself before I heard people speaking against the meetings.' He met God and knew it and was present on all possible occasions thereafter. (Roddy and the Gobha were two of the five praying men of Barvas to whom reference has been made in literature on the revival associated with Mr Campbell. Many readers will be familiar with the story of how they prayed through the night and prevailed with God before revival broke out in Barvas.) Now Roddy knew God and he knew the ways of the devil too. I remember him once remarking to me how he had observed that often the first meeting in a series could be powerful, but that on the next day he could feel the wicked one rising strongly all over the area to prevent the work of God proceeding. It was very true. I used to wonder how one could be so close to God at the end of the first night and waken the next morning feeling that God was a thousand miles away. Of course if one went on with God, He had the victory and His presence and power could come and abide.

No doubt the Gobha heard of things and became interested, but still, I imagine, did not want to be seen to be openly supporting the meetings. I think he hit on a face-saving device. I was due to hold a meeting in the home of a Mrs MacDonald in Shader and he *happened* to be visiting there one day. He just stayed on for the meeting. Whether this was intentional or accidental I never knew but I was suspicious. Maybe this is unfair for he has gone home to Glory now and can't defend himself! In any case the meeting commenced and there was the Gobha. This must have happened about thirty years ago and yet I remember it as clearly as though it had been last night.

I sat meditating before the time to preach arrived and had a very distinct impression that the Gobha had imbibed the heresy that Pentecost diverted attention from Christ and the Cross, and I felt God gave me a very clear word to deal with the situation. It is strange to feel strongly that you know what is in the mind of a man and that God wants his thoughts taken out one by one and answered.

My text was, 'Even though we have known Christ after the flesh, yet now we know Him so no more.' I spoke of the disciples having known Christ in the days of His flesh, of having been with Him daily, of having witnessed His miracles and of having listened to His teaching—and yet not knowing Him as they were to know Him after Pentecost. They did not have the inner spiritual understanding of Himself and His teaching which was later to become theirs. Indeed, immediately prior to Pentecost they were still wondering about the establishment of an earthly kingdom. Not long before that James and John had thoughts of sitting at His right hand in such an hour. Prior to Pentecost the disciples had known Him and loved Him but they were still to share His Spirit in ways they did not know.

Of the Spirit Christ said, '. . . he abideth with you, and shall be in you . . . he shall guide you into all the truth . . . he shall take of mine, and shall declare it unto you' (Jn 14:17; 16:13–14). I proceeded to show that instead of the Baptism taking attention away from Christ it very particularly concentrated it on Christ. Christ became central in actual practice and not merely in vague theory. The case was strong and the evidence was there in the Bible and also in the outworked experience of men.

I am not convinced that it swayed John Smith the Gobha one whit—but I had done what God wanted me to do and we turned to prayer as was my wont in all these meetings. These prayer times were times of seeking God that He might pour out His spirit and do His own work in the hearts of men. They were really 'waiting' times rather than prayer meetings of the type with which most evangelicals are familiar.

Suddenly God came down upon a young man and he was baptized in the Spirit. The Gobha looked like a man electrified. He swung round. He had been through revival. He recognised the moving of God. He may have been prejudiced against me but he could not deny the manifestation of God. From that hour he became my friend and attended meetings regularly—leading the singing gloriously. The young man went on to be much used of God, leading many to Christ.

As I got to know the Gobha I began to learn inner things about the '39 revival. It was he who had convened the first meetings in Shader and it was in his house that revival first broke out in that district. My information is that after the Point Communion early in '39 two people were converted on the bus coming home to Shader and the Gobha sent word to all the houses in the area announcing that he was holding a meeting. From then on, on alternate nights there were meetings in his home and in the home of Miss Barbara Macdonald (the next person to whom I will be making reference). I was amazed when he told me of the depth of Satanic opposition. He said, 'It was so awful that I became convinced that I had been mistaken in holding the meetings and I decided to end them. *It took four men to hold me down and prevent me doing this. I was saved in time. That night revival broke out.*'

Phenomena were intense and widespread. People were powerfully convicted and converted. There was great freedom amongst the Christians in prayer and worship. Glory flowed like rivers and Satan moved to destroy the work and he moved through men. Some of the greatest opposition in that area came from one of the churches and this led to confusion amongst the people and caused a great hindrance.

18

Meet Barbara and Other Prayer Warriors

I heard of Barbara long before I met her. She was bedridden and in almost constant pain. I heard of her as a woman of God—a woman who had been greatly used in prayer and in revival. One man Colin told me his story. He was addicted to drink and found himself one day, in time of revival, in a public house in Stornoway. He picked up his glass and was about to drink when suddenly Barbara Macdonald stood before him in spirit. In fear he put the glass down and left the bar. He went directly home and as he passed Barbara's house which was on the main road in Shader she stepped out before him (in the flesh this time) and he fell to his knees on the road, giving his life to Christ. He held her in great awe and respect.

An interview was arranged for me with Barbara and I was told that I might be able to see her but it would depend on the circumstances of the day. Sometimes the pain she suffered was so great she could see no one. On other days it was possible. The day came and she talked to me almost in gasps between bouts of pain. She spoke of revival. 'Ah,' she said, 'it was a wonderful time—for some people—but for us it was also a terrible time. We were not in the meetings, you know, where the people were being blessed. We were called by God to the place of prayer and we would be in another room when the meetings were going on and the power would come and we would be filled with power and the burden of prayer would grow and grow. It was like childbirth. The pangs would come and the pain would come and then there was a sense of delivery and joy as a soul was born into the kingdom (as would be happening in the other room). And then the wind would come again and the pangs and the pain and the delivery. Again and again it would come. It was very wonderful but it was very costly.' She rejoiced in the glory of those days but she left an impression on me as no one else had ever done of the real nature of intercession. I had learned much from the biographies of Charles Finney, Praying Hyde and David Brainerd, but this lady was there before me and presented the inner truth and the inner agony in a most striking way. I never burble (if I may use such a word) about prayer. Real prayer is no light, casual matter. It is a mighty weapon in the hand of a man of God. It is not to be lightly regarded—it is far removed from the vapid vapourings that so often pass for prayer in our day. Real prayer is a world removed from what many people regard as prayer acceptable to God. With its twin sister faith it is strong to pull down kingdoms and remove mountains; it is certainly critical in revival and was a vital component of the movement in Lewis in 1939.

These two, John Smith and Barbara Macdonald, were intimate friends of Mary MacLean and deeply involved with her in promoting revival in the Shader-Barvas area in 1939. Roddy Alick was of the same company and I imagine that Coinneach Beag, Mary's brother, would be with them then. I remember hearing a lovely story of Coinneach from Duncan Campbell in the later revival. Coinneach was a deeply spiritual man and a man of prayer. I think he indicated to Mr Campbell that revival would break out in Carloway at a particular time and was with him in the first meetings. There came a very hard meeting and Mr Campbell stopped preaching, sat down and called on Coinneach to pray. He stood up and began to intercede and I think he may have prayed for about half an hour. 'There came a moment,' Mr Campbell said, 'when he heard something he never heard before or after. Coinneach was speaking to God and said, 'Will you excuse me for one moment, Lord, while I speak to the devil.' Mr Campbell opened his eyes to see Coinneach with his fists raised as a fighting man and he addressed the devil to some purpose. I think he demanded that he go from the place. Suddenly it was like the bursting of an atom bomb in the church. God flooded in. Revival had come. The devil was expelled and God reigned. 'At such a moment,' Mr Campbell said, 'I sat down and the Holy Spirit did His own work.' The story had an amusing tailpiece. 'The next time I saw Coinneach,' Mr Campbell continued, 'he was stretched out on a bench fast asleep.' The meeting was still going on but Coinneach's work was done and he slept the sleep of the just.

A final tailpiece. The thought of a 'half-hour prayer' may shake a weaker generation. The length of many a Highland prayer would—but, in fact, when prayer is under deep anointing it is glorious and never tedious. When the Spirit, however, is absent and the prayer lengthy it can be very difficult and indeed harmful. In one locality (which I feel it wise not to name) Mr Campbell once said that the first meetings were at least partly spoiled by the long prayers of the elders (and supposing four prayed you could have two solid hours of prayer which might be largely in the flesh). Mr Campbell feared that the coming of revival was endangered and being a man of character took action. Perhaps he had heard the story of Moody and Grenfell of Labrador. When the latter was a young man he went into a Moody meeting where a gentleman was praying all round the world. The young man was about to leave just as Moody intervened saying, 'We'll sing a hymn while our brother finishes his prayer.' Grenfell thought a man who had the character to do this might be worth waiting to hear preach. He waited and found Christ that day and eventually became a much-used missionary in Labrador. Mr Campbell found his own novel solution to his problem. He arrived one night and announced, 'I had always thought that the men of ——————— were godly men but I see I have been mistaken. In my view, a godly man is a man who spends so much time in private prayer that when he comes to church he has very little left to say.' From that night, as you may well imagine, the prayers were short and revival came in power.

I have allowed myself to digress because I feel that stories can be interesting and much is often remembered through a story that would otherwise be forgotten. I am aware that I sometimes break strict literary convention in my writing but that may be no bad thing either! In earlier years in my profession I knew and followed the rules and kept within the bounds. Now I am free and can let a story unfold as it will, without too great a regard to accepted usage.

Such, then, were the friends of Mary MacLean who is now about to take the stage.

Like most spiritual people Mary often keeps inner spiritual things very private, but she has always wanted to see Christ glorified and has willingly consented to my telling at least some part of her story. Much I have remembered from earlier years—but for greater detail and depth I have recently visited Lewis again and taken a tape recording as she spoke of her experiences of God. Much she reveals, but of her own sufferings she says very little and perhaps I should say a word or two about these.

In the first years of her spiritual life Mary was idyllically happy—and I really mean idyllically happy; so happy that I think she thought she was going quickly home to Heaven

. . . but the days were to change. I do not know that I have ever met anyone who has endured more suffering than has this lady. I do not want to go into all her domestic pain as well as her conflicts with hell—but I have noticed it has been with her as with so many whom God greatly uses in inner work: there is a heavy price to pay. Where Satan can rend, he will, and many of the greatest saints have, before their days on earth ended, been the greatest sufferers.

Very recently Mary lost a daughter in extremely tragic circumstances—but when we met and spoke of Christ I met a godly, indomitable spirit, totally loyal to her God. Nothing has moved her from her place in Christ. I will let her speak for herself.

I should perhaps say that Mary speaks both Gaelic and English but she thinks in Gaelic. In speaking of spiritual experience, therefore, she tended to translate for my benefit. This resulted in English with quaint features and I have put the story partly in my words and partly in hers; where her exact words are quoted I employ italics; where I felt I had to tell the story I have tried to write in tune with her own style of speech.

I trust that the story, which has unusual features, will interest readers. I should perhaps also mention that the circle of friends—Barbara, The Gobha, Roddy Alick and Coinneach Beag—are now at home with the Lord. I felt that if I did not get detail down at this time I might be too late. When the fourscore years are past it is wise not to take risks. I wanted my writing to be checked for accuracy by someone who was on the spot during the '39 revival and those who were involved in 1939 are now becoming hard to find. There is perhaps one other of the circle whom I should mention who is still alive—Miss Jessie Smith of Borve. She is a very old lady now and is in a home in Stornoway. She had a remarkable ability to know the future and even in old age this persists. Very recently in the home she saw two deaths before they took place. (I think she hoped one of them might be her own. A day or two ago she was seriously asking me if it was a sin for her to ask God to take her.)

Jessie lived with her sister Catherine (now deceased) and they were women of prayer and deeply involved in revival. On one memorable occasion during revival they were out so much at meetings that their cow went dry. For those without a farming background let me explain. If a cow stops being milked regularly her lactation ceases. There was no question with the sisters. They arranged their priorities and milking had no chance against revival!

Another lady of my acquaintance who supplied me with some of my material was absent from Lewis for most of the time revival was moving, but had at least brief contact with it. I met her some thirty years or so ago and can never forget the occasion. I was presenting Pentecost for the first time in a particular parish in Lewis. A goodly company had gathered—many of them regular attenders at the particular house meeting; others came for the occasion. One of my own party who had remarkable spiritual insight told me of her sense of Christ coming as though hurriedly into the room. There was danger. I spoke in what was a very hard atmosphere. I had personal liberty but every word seemed to bounce back from the walls. I ended and felt rather flat. The visitors departed and suddenly the lady first mentioned rose and with her hands lifted up to Heaven shouted at the pitch of her voice: 'The heavens are brass!' Three times she shouted it. I had never heard anything like it and wondered if I should intervene (southern notions of order and all that). There was neither need nor opportunity. I was standing with my back to a chiffonier and talk about the twinkling of an eye! It was faster than that. Suddenly I was full of the Spirit. I opened my eyes and prophesied. The room was like a battlefield. God had come. One girl bringing in tea felt as though her knees turned to water. Power came on a lady sitting next to the leader (husband of the lady who had shouted) and I went over and laid hands on her. The lady was known in the area for her holy walk with God. She was gloriously baptized and she fell across the man's knees. His face was a study. It registered interest, astonishment, delight and maybe concern. Ultimately he extricated himself from what may have been an embarrassing situation and crossed the room where the scene was repeated. Again a lady beside him was baptized in the Spirit speaking in tongues and she too collapsed across his knees in the opposite direction. That night his wife herself and another received the Baptism after the meeting.

This lady had been used in revival when Mr Campbell had been in the parish some time earlier. She, with her husband, endured much opposition after the events described above, but she is still going on with God, and when I saw her very recently she was out in the Spirit gloriously before I left her home; and her husband has recently experienced a lovely healing. To this lady too I am indebted for her knowledge of the '39 revival.

19

A Chosen Vessel

Mary MacLean was born into a Free Church family in Lewis in 1905. From her earliest days she was strangely drawn to the things of God. She loved to be with Christian people and was intensely interested in spiritual things. As elders and deacons were in her Grannie's home she listened closely to their conversation after meetings, delighting in hope of salvation and Heaven.

I remember once, when I was very young, bringing tea to the company when one of the elders asked another if he thought Christians would recognise each other in Heaven. I remember, as though it was yesterday, putting down the cups to hear the answer and thinking how wonderful it would be if the Lord's people would know each other. The second elder thought they would if they had been close to each other on earth. [At this point your author remembered, perhaps a little irreverently, the remark of another on this same question: 'We recognise each other on earth—surely you don't think we'll be greater fools in Heaven than we are here!']

I always envied the Lord's people and wanted to be one of them as far back as I can remember.

Mary had an unusually unworldly outlook and clearly remembers two concerts and her reaction to them. Now a concert in a country part of Lewis in those days was quite an event and had a great fascination for the young folk. Mary had left school and had gone to the first, and just could not understand its attraction for people. The second one was held in the schoolhouse and she went again simply to please others.

I wasn't interested, and I didn't know why I remained so uninterested when other young people were so interested. When I left the concert that night, I knew I would never go to a concert again. There was nothing there for me.

In those days we used to go out with the cattle to the moor[1] and a girl gave me an English New Testament to read as I had time and quietness. She promised to test me in what I read. This may have encouraged me, but I remember wishing all the time that I was a Christian.

One night a Mr. Macmillan, a missionary, came and one of my cousins was converted and she cried and cried her eyes out. Some people seemed to be so upset as the knowledge of the broken law came on them. I used to envy those people: they were so sure of their conversion. But things weren't like that with me. My own conversion was as though a child was awakened out of sleep. I didn't cry, I wasn't getting law and hard things and I wasn't sure of my conversion. I envied these others and wished I had had an experience like them.
[AUTHOR: I think this is peculiarly sweet. This young girl was unusually innocent and clean, and her awakening was a gentle and beautiful experience—there is something about this which is so like what God would do.]

At sixteen Mary left home and went into service in Glasgow, where she would no doubt be exposed to the temptations of the big city. She seems, however, to have been peculiarly guarded. A very pure spirituality seems to have been around her like a cloak. To her, a temptation did not need to be gross to be resisted. It might seem no more than an innocent pastime—but she was very sensitive to seemingly legitimate things that might lure her away from her spiritual quest for God.

I had a cousin in Glasgow who took me one night to the Highlandman's Umbrella.[2] *I said to myself, 'If I get out of this I'll never come back again.' I didn't say it to my cousin, who was older than I, but I was determined that if I got back to Professor Muir's house where I was a cook, I would never visit the Highlandman's Umbrella again.* [AUTHOR: Mary doesn't say quite what happened—but no doubt the remarks of the gathered throng would not be to her taste. While many Highland folk are deeply Christian, many others are very deeply not so!]

I attended the Partick Highland Free Church in Glasgow. When church came out it was the custom for the young people to meet on the Great Western Road. A friend met me one night at the door of the church after the service and said, 'We'll go up to the Great Western Road. Everyone goes there after the meeting.' I didn't like to refuse, although at the time I was seeking the Lord and not getting through. When I got to the Great Western Road I was ashamed of myself—thinking the boys would be thinking that we were after them [AUTHOR: which the boys no doubt were, and in which they were in the main correct!]. *'Ah well,' I said, 'If I get home tonight I'm not coming here again. I will go straight home after church. I will never go to the Great Western Road again.' When I refused to go with the others they would say, 'Och, you're converted, you're converted.' 'No,' I would say, 'I am not converted.' 'Then why won't you go?' 'There's nothing for me there. I don't see what interests you there. It has no interest for me, so I won't go.'*

It is a wonder I was not burned alive in those days. I would go to bed and, not wanting to have to get up later and put out the gas, I would take a candle and put it on the pillow as I read my Bible and sought God in prayer. One night I fell asleep and when I awoke there was nothing left of the candle but a very small stump. I never did that again.

I had a half-day each week and I wanted to spend this with Christians, but didn't know where to go, and was afraid that if

I did find such company I would spoil things for them. Since I was not through to God I was afraid that I would prevent them getting through too.

One day, as I read my Bible at the part where Christ asks: 'Are ye come out, as against a robber, with swords and staves to seize me?' (Mk 14:48), I felt I was like the chief of sinners crucifying Christ. It was five years before I confessed the Lord, going forward to the table for Communion.

The Rev. Peter Chisholm was my minister in Partick Highland Free Church, and he was my favourite preacher. He came down very hard on all forms of sin and I appreciated this. He stirred me and I wanted to be stirred. At last the day came when I got through fully with the Lord. I was on my knees washing the floor when God spoke to me from Ephesians 2:13–14: 'But now in Christ Jesus ye that once were far off are made nigh in the blood of Christ. For he is our peace, who made both one, and brake down the middle wall of partition.' I got through on that verse, but then Satan came and said, 'Nobody ever got through on her knees washing a floor.' That's how I was tempted—it was as if Satan had a grip on my clothes all the time; he said, 'You're not going to get away.' Now I had a friend from Lochs, and she came out with me to the Saturday Communion service. She said, 'Mary, we're going to the session tonight to go forward for Christ.' 'Jessie Maggie,' I said, 'Don't depend on me. The Lord alone knows what I will do tonight. But don't go by me. If you are ready to go into the session, go in . . . but don't depend on me. Go on your own. The Lord alone knows what I will do tonight.' It was Mr. Chisholm who started the service that night: which was unusual since it was his own Communion and normally it was a visiting minister who took this service. I said in my heart, 'Thank the Lord that it's you that's going to be preaching tonight, and you'll search me thoroughly; you won't leave anything untouched.' So that was that. And as he was going on with the service, at one time I would think, 'I will go forward . . . I think I'm getting through all right'—and then a wave of doubt would come. In any case, when the service was finished, he said, as everyone says at the end, 'And those now that want to come forward tomorrow for the table, the session is open for the last time. And you,' he said as he was pointing to me, 'And you who are here tonight before me saying that you don't belong to Christ wherever you put your handwriting, don't say, "No," when Christ says, "Yes." ' And when he said this, he struck his hand on the pulpit. I went past him. I got it there, and I got to a stage when I was no longer worried about what Mr. Chisholm might question me on. I was past thinking of him; I was going forward for Christ that night. It was not the minister now, but Christ. When I went out, there was no sign of my girl-friend, Jessie Maggie. An elder came forward to take me into the session. And all the minister asked was, what had made me come in tonight? and I said I wanted to go as far for Christ as I could. And he didn't ask anything else. He gave me the token and he prayed. 'You'll now go straight on,' he said. But after I left the church, Satan came. 'Chisholm knew,' he said, 'that you had nothing to answer tonight: that's why he didn't put the questions—the deep questions you were thinking he was going to ask. He knew that you had nothing. And the token he gave you tonight— he'll be in the door waiting for you to take it away tomorrow.' 'Oh well, God knows I am not worthy of going for Communion. That's all right. That's all right.'

It was on the night after this that I got wonderful light. I had to be in that night. And when I went to sleep, I saw Christ with His hands raised, saying: 'Father, that which thou has given me, I will that, where I am, they also may be with me' (Jn 17:24). It was His voice that awoke me, and oh, it was so loud. And when I looked, He was gone. And I didn't know the bedroom; I didn't know where I was. I could only hear singing of birds, and I wasn't hearing trams or cars or anything like that; I didn't know the bedroom at all. And I thought I was going to die; I thought I was going to Heaven.

This was the beginning of vision for me. When I got up, I

was still thinking the Lord was going to take me away. And a Christian girl from Ness, from the Church of Scotland, was next door to me. And as soon as I got the dishes washed in the morning, I went round to see her. And she asked me, 'Oh, Mary, why have you come so early as this?' 'Oh, Christine, I'm going to die,' I said. 'Everyone's going to die,' she replied. 'What's wrong, Mary?' I told her of the vision I'd seen of Christ and of the words He spoke to me and the peace I was feeling, and that I was sure I was going to die. 'You, my dear, go home and do all you have to do. You have to go through a lot before you get away from this world. Go now and do everything you have to do in the house.' And so I did. And the peace was wonderful. It was as if I was walking on air for two years . . . it was a wonderful time. Jessie Maggie, the girl I told to go forward for Communion if she was ready for it and not go by what I did, waited for another two years. No-one went forward that time but myself.

This happened when I was twenty-three years old — sixty years ago. [AUTHOR: From this time till the revival in 1939, Mary enjoyed the presence of the Lord continuously. She knew His presence and His power.] *I had the presence of the Lord all the time, the power of the Spirit all the time.*

Notes

[1] In the Highlands, people often went in the summer to the shielings and stayed there for weeks at a time. Shielings were very simple temporary houses and may still be seen dotted here and there in the heather. Many readers will recall the lovely lines about the Highlander far away on another shore, remembering the land of his birth:

> From the lone shieling of the misty island
> Mountains divide us and the waste of seas—
> Yet still the blood is strong, the heart is Highland
> And we in dreams behold the Hebrides. . .

[2] A famous gathering place in past years for Highland folk. It was that part of Argyll Street which is under the railway. People were often poor, and the place was free and dry. It had become a custom to gather there on Sundays.

20

Visions Before Revival

I have found in Lewis a great quickening of spiritual
faculties. In a peculiar way the veil between this world and
the spiritual world seems to be very thin. God and the
things of God become very real. The sense of evil too at
times can be intense. One has the feeling of moving in a
very elemental world. Some people from the south have
visited the Island and gone home greatly blessed. Others
have been glad to get away, having brushed against evil in
a frightening way. Thirty years ago I used to think that
places like Lewis were a hundred years nearer God and
reality than the supposedly more advanced southern
regions. They had the blessing of being without the disad-
vantages of television and were behind the times in the
disco pop scene. Life was very close to nature and the
people met often in each others' homes. Christians often
had house gatherings. Non-Christians had their ceilidhs.
Much of this has now changed and television has the same
kind of dominating influence there as it has in most other
parts—reducing the time people meet in a quiet, social,
communicating context, and also gradually imposing

standards of its own. Even so, I noticed on a recent visit to the Island that spirituality is not dead—it may be slumbering in many places, but it is there to be roused. It may be that there is something in the character of the people that distinguishes them. It is certainly true that when the Spirit of God begins to move there are sensitive people who respond deeply. For myself, I find God at depth there and unfailingly come back invigorated—even after a very brief stay and even after a very heavy programme of activity. It is a spiritual land and amongst its inhabitants are some very spiritual people. Conversion is not regarded lightly. It is a deep, life-changing experience and a converted person is expected to show clear evidence of it in his life. It is no mere external profession of faith. The church still exerts a powerful, though perhaps now a declining, influence. Ungodliness and addiction to alcohol is the other side of the coin, and many are in these categories too.

It is against this background that I want you to read of some of the visions of Mary MacLean. She comes of a people who are given to vision: and vision is not a strange matter to this people. She lives in a land where the veil is thin and she has led a peculiarly godly life. She has been, in fact, a prepared vessel. As we noted in the last chapter, she had a lovely vision and an out-of-the-body experience shortly after her first Communion. We go on now to a vision which came immediately prior to the Second World War, and which seems to have been related to it.

On the 10th of March, 1939, Mary had a baby daughter, and she felt herself very strongly surrounded by the presence of God. Two nights later the first vision came. *There came a rushing wind. I was away. I don't know how long I was away—but the graves opened—the graves opened, and I thought it was the last day—Judgment Day. I don't know how long I was away, but when I came back I said, 'O Lord, if it's Judgment Day, everyone here is unconverted.' And the* power came for praying for all those unconverted persons all over the world. The whole world came upon me. And I was shaking, and I prayed that I would go away again. I was just waiting like that. And there came the rushing wind again. I was away. It was the sea that came in front of me then. And I went down to the bottom of the sea. And the ships were lying there, and the bodies of men were lying there. Oh, what a place! I don't know how long I was away, but when I came back I was shaking, and Baby was beside me. When the war broke out in August, that was when I got a revelation about the place of seeing when I was down at the bottom of the sea and saw the bodies there. 'Well,' I thought, 'This is the war now that I have seen, the ships down there in pieces, and the bodies.' I was afraid that I would go away again, and wondered what I would see next—what would be revealed to me? But I didn't go away then and decided not to tell anyone of anything I had seen. They would think that the Lord was going to take me away, and they would be so upset.

Now the Communions were coming about the 15th of March, and Baby was born on the 10th. I would preach to the unconverted that a revival was on its way. I told them to be out day and night at the meetings at Communion time and not to miss anything, that a great revival was coming. And, oh, they were thinking something was wrong with me—they didn't know what was coming upon me: 'Oh, be out, be out morning and night,' I said. Pressure was coming upon me, and prayer was coming. I thought the Lord was going to take me home, and I wasn't worried for the family; I knew the Lord would get someone to look after the family. I was all prepared to be taken away—oh, the presence of the Lord was so strong, I thought no-one could stay in this cold world without the presence of the Lord. And there was a girl who lived near me, and she used to help me with the baby. 'Oh, Hetty,' I used to say, 'Be out morning and evening. Revival's going to come.' And after the Communions she came and said, 'I was out every morning and every night, and no revival came.' 'The revival is coming,' I said. 'You keep out. The revival is coming.' Anyway, the Communions in Point came about the end of March. And I was waiting for the revival, when the power would come.

21

Revival and the Outbreak of War

Two people were converted in the bus coming over from Point to Barvas at the end of the Communions. The Gobha was there. And when the Gobha got home he sent two wee girls to every house that evening, saying that he was going to hold a meeting, and that he was inviting everyone. My husband wasn't converted at the time. And he was planting potatoes, when he saw the two girls at the door and came up and asked who they were. 'The Gobha has sent two girls inviting everyone to a meeting in his house tonight,' I said. 'Oh, yes, but it's not the likes of me the Gobha is inviting, but Christians.' 'No,' I said, and the pressure came on me, 'You have to go. You have to go to the meeting.' And when he saw the pressure coming on me, he was afraid and he said, 'All right, I'll go.' And he went to the meeting that night.

'What now about the meeting?' I said, when he came home.

'One thing about the meeting is that I am thankful you were not out in the meeting.' 'Why?' I said. 'I know you would have been one of the chief among them. Some were standing singing, some were falling down on the floor, and some others were preaching away, preaching away: and you would have been among them. And I'm thankful you could not go out, that you are not able to be out, with the baby.'

'Well,' I said, 'Never you mind. All you have to do is close your eyes and leave everything you hear and see and just pray to God, "O Lord, open my eyes and gain my heart for yourself," and ignore everything you hear and see: don't be offended with anything you see, but pray away for your soul.'

'Oh, well, I am thankful you are not among them, and I'm not going tomorrow night.' 'Yes, you have to go. You have to go now.' 'All right,' he said, 'All right. I'll go all right.' He went out that night.

'What now about the meeting?' I asked, when he came home. (When the power came on me in the house here, I was forced to go on my knees. The power of prayer came on me for the meeting, and for the coming of revival to open the hearts of the unconverted. The burden wasn't just for one or two, but for the whole world.) My husband said, 'Oh, they were worse tonight than they were last night. Only I'm thankful that the baby's here to keep you in the house.' That was his story each night—'. . . thankful that the baby's here and that you'll not be able to be there.'

And the third night, I didn't ask him to go. He went without my asking. And when he came home, I didn't venture to ask what was going on. I knew something was happening; I felt it. And when he took the Book[1], to say prayers, the tears were running down from his eyes, and I never asked about the meeting. I saw that he had been converted.

By this time, meetings were being held in two houses (Barbara Macdonald's and the Gobha's) and Mary very much wanted to go, but because of the baby's being breastfed there were difficulties. The power came frequently on Barbara, and her mother kept her away from Mary lest she too went again under the power to the extent of being unable to cope with the baby.

But when they heard that I too was under the power, Barbara was allowed in. The power was great. The revival had come.

But Satan came too. Satan had his own power among the

people. Oh, yes. When I would send anyone for the young people to come in, I used to preach to them, and when my younger brother came in among the others, he would say, 'Mary, we don't know who to believe.' The young people were going to the meeting, to Barbara's meeting and to the Gobha's. Some were saying it was the devil's work, and some were saying it was the Lord's. Wasn't it remarkable that some members were saying it was Satan's work? And the poor unconverted souls were standing between the two groups: between Satan and the Lord's work. And that was so hard. And the pressure for prayer for the Church of God came upon us now so heavily: the pressure for the people who were saying it was the devil's work. And there were ministers too against the revival. The minister in our church was against it—but not in the neighbouring Church of Scotland. Oh, the battle I have gone through with that minister and the elders. I'll never forget it. But I was standing in the power of the Lord. And I wasn't afraid; I was telling everything that the Lord was doing. And there I was, I had to stay in. But when Baby grew well on in months, I used to go to the Church of Scotland meetings here. War came and my husband went away, and I was here with the family. I wasn't able to go out much . . . but when I got a chance I would go to the Church of Scotland.

I had then started going into visions again. Some of them were long visions and I needed my mother's help to look after the baby. It wouldn't have been possible for me to attend to her myself, for the length and depth of the visions. The longest vision[2] I've been in was one in which I went cold, as cold as if I were dead. And, oh, the vision I saw there, a vision of Heaven, and of hell. And hell—there was a plunging into hell as if sheep were plunging over a precipice, and I was hearing the gnashing of teeth and the crying. I saw the flames going through the people (the flames were not burning up and down the way, but going through them across the way). And I thought, with the furnace that was coming out of hell, that there wasn't a hair on my head that wasn't singed with the furnace.[3]

*But then, a vision of Heaven, and Christ . . . . I couldn't
take my eyes off Him . . . I couldn't blink. And the vision of
Heaven was so wonderful. And the brightest day here is like
darkness compared with the light that's there in Heaven.*

*And I was away so far, my sister told my mother, 'Mary has
passed away, and you must believe that Mary won't come back
now. She's gone cold, and I have taken out clothes to put on
her now, and white sheets that'll go over her in the bed, until
the coffin comes.' My sister was so upset. I was just cold, as
cold as a dead body. I don't remember now how long my
mother said I was away. But a crowd was in the house,
thinking that I had passed away and that the wake was going
to be on. And there was one in Lower Shader, a very dear soul
that was under the power like myself. She was my cousin. And
her brother, an elder in the Free Church, was in. And he went
home and told her, 'Annie, you won't see Mary now again.
Mary has passed away.' Annie didn't believe that I had
passed away. And my sister told my mother, 'You must believe
Mary has passed away this time.' 'No, I don't believe Mary
has passed away. I have often seen Mary going away like this,
going away like this.' 'Oh, but not like this, Mum. She's stone
cold; every bit of her is stone cold, and there's no pulse that we
can find.'*

*Anyway, after that (I don't know how long, but I was a
good while away), I felt streams going through my body,
through my arms, and through every bit of me, like thin streams
warming me up. And when I got a bit warmed up, I said to my
sister, 'Oh, Annie, will you bring me a hot water bottle?' And
Annie said that that was the most wonderful thing she ever
heard. I couldn't move at this stage, I couldn't move my arms
or my legs. But bit by bit I was warming up. My right arm
warmed first. And when I got as far as putting my arm to my
brow it was like putting a hand on a dead body. My head was
still cold. But everything else was warm. And I came back to
life.*

My mother asked me when she saw I was fully back, 'Oh,

Mary, did you see anything about our own house?' 'Well, I didn't see anything, but I know this, that you're going to be left alone.' The war hadn't broken out then. Later my three brothers were taken to the war, and we were left alone then. 'I have seen that you are going to be alone in the house.' And she couldn't understand how that would happen. Where were the boys going—the three of them? but they were taken to the war in August. And I was with my mother all the time. And it was when the war broke out that I realised that what I had seen in vision down at the bottom of the sea, with the ships and the bodies all about, was connected with the war.

Just before war broke out I was finally able to come home with the children; my husband and my three brothers were taken away to the war. One night I was on my knees praying for my brothers and for everyone in the world. I saw the ship the youngest one was in; it was a trawler. It was in half—it was split in half, and I saw him in the water. With what I saw I got up from my knees and started thinking, 'Och, it must have been that I was praying for him and was afraid that this would happen.' And I started walking the floor. Oh, what was this? what was this? Anyway, word that he was missing came, and I told people that this happened two weeks ago (the night was clear in my memory). The postman left letters here for me to break it to my father and mother. He was missing. But then word came that he wasn't found among the survivors. And I told them, 'Well, this happened two weeks ago.' They said, 'How do you know that?' 'I've seen it,' I said, 'I've seen it with my eyes. I know this.'

Next, my other brother died on board his ship, with, I think, a gastrated stomach. There was a month between them, that was all. And he was buried at sea. Seemingly he had been converted. He had talked to a man from Carloway who was with him on the boat, a Christian. He had said, 'When we get home after the war, you'll go down to our house, so that it will be easier for me to go out to the weekly meetings with you.[4]

Soon after that, an urge came on me to go back to my own church, at a Communion time. And I said, 'O Lord, I can't go there. How can I go there? I have not been going to that church, and how can I venture out at the Communions?' But the pressure of the Lord came, and I had to go. But I wouldn't do this without going first to the elders and saying that I was forced to take Communion.

'Oh, well,' they said, 'You'll have to come in before the elders and before the minister.'

Oh, what a position! But mind you, I wasn't afraid. I was going to tell them the truth, and the power that was coming upon me. I wasn't afraid about whether they would turn me back without getting to the Communion table; that wasn't going to worry me. But Christ couldn't say that I didn't go as far as I could. The responsibility would be on them. The minister asked me why I was going out to the Church of Scotland, and wouldn't come to my own church.

'Because you wouldn't allow us in there: you wouldn't allow any who were under the power of the Spirit to come in. And I didn't want to spoil anything, or to upset anyone; so I was keeping away from you.'

'And do you promise to come if you get to the table?'

'Well, I'll promise, if the Lord gives me the strength to come to the church, I'll come. But if not, I can't come.' I also said to the elders, 'None of you, none of the elders, came to see us during the meetings. And the ministers didn't come to see us during the meetings, during the time when we were under the power of the Spirit. None of you were coming to see us.'

'Oh,' the elders said, 'you are right, Mrs. MacLean, none of us went to see you. Well, you'll go forward the same as you ever did.'

And so I did go to the table. But the power came after that, and I couldn't venture out to this church. And at every opportunity I had to go, I went back to the Church of Scotland. And mind you, what a battle: you can understand what I was going through. But the power was so strong from the Lord, and the presence of the Lord was so wonderful, and I was saying, 'Oh, well, as long as I am under this pressure, the Lord will give me all the words I need. I don't need to worry.' I stayed in at the next Communion. And do you know, I was so much under the power that the Communion bread and wine were brought to me here.

At the next Communion the Lord's presence and power came strongly and I had to go again. I wasn't afraid, and I was prepared to speak openly to the elders in front of the minister. And the minister asked, 'Why didn't you come to the church after you had Communion?'

'Because when the power came upon me I was going out of the body and I didn't want to upset any of you. When the power of the Spirit came on me I was going off, and it was there I was seeing the visions.' They made no comment on this. 'Oh, well, you can come any time you feel the Lord is leading you to come to the table!' So that was my experience with them.[5]

Notes

[1] A Highland expression for the family reading of the Bible.
[2] This one came just before the war.
[3] Mary also indicated that far more were going into hell than into Heaven—just as Christ predicted in His reference to the broad and narrow ways.
[4] This, from a Highland point of view, was an almost certain sign that he had been converted.
[5] I understand that the minister and elders of Mary's church objected to the manifestations that were evident when the power of God came upon His servants in particular ways. A person on whom the power fell during a church service might be physically removed. This explains Mary's reluctance to going to her own church.

22

Miscellanea

I interrupted Mary's story to question her closely about some of her visions, and she clarified the following points. Evidently she was out of the body on and off for most of a fortnight on the occasion when she was thought to be dead.

In the vision in which she saw Christ standing between Heaven and hell and was unable to take her eyes off Him, the dead whom she saw go into Heaven and hell were the war dead from her own area.

She identified the house in which she was when news of the fall of France was broadcast on the radio. The news profoundly depressed the company who were gathered. God gave her very clear knowledge of the outcome of events. She threw up her hands and glorified God, indicating that France had to fall before victory could come. She saw the defeat of Germany and the ultimate triumph of the Allies. At first the company were astounded at her glorifying God at the news of the fall of France and wondered if they had a traitor in their midst but, as Mary explained future events, the power and presence of God evidently became very strong and the whole company were affected and shared in the joy. It was a very wonderful night.

Mary went on to corroborate what Barbara had told me of the costly nature of prayer in the time of revival—where she likened spiritual birth to natural birth with birth pangs for those bearing the burden as souls were born into the Kingdom.

People were divided during the revival. There were those who were powerfully affected and those who opposed it and never came into it; and in the later revival under Mr Campbell it was largely those who had been in the '39 revival who gave support. Others who had resisted in 1939 still generally remained outside of the moving.[1]

Mary is of the opinion that the '39 revival was more powerful than the later one and may in a sense have conditioned it.

There were many converts during the '39 revival and, before the counter-attack came, Mary had been hopeful that the whole community would be converted. The attack did not come from the unconverted but from within her own church. Had the leaders moved with God, she feels that the outcome would have been even more glorious.

Mary confirmed the story of Calan a Bhucaich (Colin Macleod) to which reference was made earlier. Colin was the man who was in the pub in Stornoway when he saw Barbara in vision and put down his glass and made his way home to be confronted by her on the street—where he fell to his knees and was converted.

I was particularly interested to get more detail on Mary's vision of Heaven and proceeded on a question and answer basis:

HBB: Now what else can I get out of you?—a wee bit more about the vision of Heaven. Can you put the vision of Heaven into clear words?

MMCL: *The vision of Heaven . . . Heaven is such, that the brightest day on earth is only like dawn, compared to that brightness.*

HBB: Like twilight, do you mean?

MMCL: *Like twilight. Like twilight, compared with the day that's going to come. Yes, the day that's going to come. But it was Christ I was seeing between the two places, and the sun— the place behind, with Him there, was so bright, oh, so bright, so bright. Oh, yes, so bright.*

AHB: Did you feel you were able to look without being dazzled?

MMCL: *Well, how I remember it is that I couldn't move my eyes at all.*

Another interesting snippet I gleaned related to the later revival. Many will have heard of the famous concert in Carloway that was interrupted by Mr McLennan in order to explain that the piper who was supposed to have been coming had been converted. The piper, Willie Smith, was Mary's eldest daughter's husband. The M.C. of the dance, Allan Macarthur, and his parents were converted shortly afterwards.

Mary confirmed that she had been speaking in tongues during the '39 revival, but not again until we met on one of my early visits to Lewis. She used almost exactly the famous words spoken by Peter on the day of Pentecost when he quoted Joel: *This is that*, as she compared her experience that day to what had happened to her so many years before.

She went on to speak appreciatively of the close fellowship she has enjoyed with a number of our own folks and their friends. Of two of these[2] she commented appreciatively: *Always I can get through with them both in my prayers. With most people I cannot.* Gratefully I heard her speak of her fellowship with myself: *As for Mr. Black, I am with him always in my prayers, day and night. I wake up during the night praying for him.* Mary's faithfulness in this through the years is not a thing taken for granted by me— but to have such a person uphold me I count as one of the great privileges of my life.

I discovered that she has read the books I have already published with great care and one of her comments gave me real pleasure: *They give me an opening to God*. That is exactly what I want them to do for all readers. She spoke of the aloneness which she and others who share her experience often find. They have God, but fellowship on earth is restricted. The deep inner things can only be shared by a limited circle. I suppose the further a people get away from revival the more real does this divide become. Spiritual things are spiritually discerned and spiritually understood. Without depth of experience a whole world remains closed. People who understand Mary, or the realm in which her spirit dwells, are not over-plentiful in our day.

An interesting discussion followed on the agelessness of spirituality. Mary herself has retained, I might almost say, the joy and a certain vivacity of youth. She is a very stable and serene person. There is no false excitement about her—but rather the feeling that 'still waters run deep.' She has not grown old with the passing of the years, neither in a sense has age wearied her. At a human level, yes, there have been sorrow and trials—but the indestructible spirit shines brightly.

I have been fascinated by this phenomenon in deeply spiritual lives. I remember being particularly struck with the late David du Plessis. On the one occasion when I heard him preach I felt I was looking at an outward shell which was gossamer thin, and behind it lay a spirit shining in light about to wing its way to its eternal home. In no way had it grown old or jaded. It radiated glorious life. If I may diverge as memories come back . . . . He taught that John the Baptist's words, 'He shall thoroughly purge his threshing floor,' should be understood as referring to the Baptism in the Spirit and not to a future judgment. I recommend the view to readers for your serious consideration. I have often noticed that a mighty purging—a purging thorough by Christ's standards—does take place in association with true Baptism in the Spirit. The dross surely does get burned up. This does not mean of course that there will not be similar happenings in a future day of judgment.

Another memory of du Plessis also related to the Baptism, about which he was preaching at the time. 'Notice,' he said, 'that in water baptism the last part of a man to go under is his head. So it often is with the Baptism in the Spirit.' How often the mind holds out against the experience and is the last to go under.

I remember too du Plessis' experience similar to Philip's when the Lord caught the latter away and he was found at Azotus. As I looked at David that day I could well believe the miracle. He seemed to me to be almost in another world as he spoke. He was then an old man but seemed more alive than many a youth of twenty. Surely the spirit does not grow old!

We spoke of Satanic attack. Mary commented: *I never shook. I wasn't going to change, whoever came against me, a minister or elder or anything; I was going to be straightforward, having the Lord's presence with me, helping to give me the words I had to speak. It was strange that I was never afraid to meet those who opposed me. I was never worried by this. The Lord was giving me the words to say.*

There followed a reference to Satan's early attack on her after her conversion. God had given her assurance of His acceptance from Ephesians 2:13–14: 'But now in Christ Jesus ye that once were far off are made nigh in the blood of Christ. For he is our peace, who made both one, and brake down the middle wall of partition.' This happened as she washed the floor and Satan tried to upset her with the idea that nobody ever got her peace washing a floor. This reminded me of some of the most glorious moments of my own life when Christ was intimately close. In my case it was cleaning out a piggery—which I may say was much in need of cleaning! I was so deeply in Christ that I was almost ecstatic. There was great persecution at the time because of my recent Pentecostal experience—but the joy of the Lord was indescribable.

Mary went on to refer to the verse she got on the first day she met me. Before I arrived (and she had no knowledge of my coming) God spoke to her. The verse from my point of view was very encouraging—but I have always kept it private from friends and family. They, of course, have shown more interest in finding this out than in learning of many other matters. It reminds me of a lovely story of a friend. There were children in the house where he was staying and at Christmas a calendar arrived, one of whose pictures seemed unsuitable for young eyes. It was removed with no explanation. In due time the family were in another home where the same calendar was hanging on the wall. The children made a bee-line for the calendar. They were totally uninterested in every picture in the calendar except the one which was missing from their own.

I remember meeting this same kind of dilemma as a headmaster. There was one set of material I wanted to introduce for Guidance lessons—but there was one section which I found objectionable. To ask that it be omitted from lessons would focus particular attention on it. To say nothing meant that it would be presented and in all probability largely forgotten. Could I be morally responsible for this?—there lay the dilemma—and it tends to be a recurring kind of dilemma.

Well, there is an amusing side to the Mary story. I had one of my daughters with me as I interviewed Mary and other old friends in Lewis with a view to writing this book—and the verse that God had given with reference to my first meeting Mary came tumbling out—much to my daughter's amusement. It was duly included in the transcript from the tape, but I am still not prepared to have it made public!

Mary spoke of the unity of spirit which she has had with me over all the years and spoke of another with whom this was similar. It was the Rev. Peter Chisholm—her minister when she was converted. She held him in great respect. He was evidently a very effective preacher. He held his people to a very high standard. This Mary obviously greatly approved. She told one or two very interesting stories about him.

He was making new elders. And he said, a week before it happened, that he was going to have new elders, and, 'It's as well for us to try to build the wall with turf seeing we haven't got stones!' One missionary told me, 'I haven't gone out since he gave that verse.' 'Oh, your pride. Nothing keeps you from going to hear him but your pride alone. But you have to go and hear him.' But he stayed in a few weeks, and Chisholm[3] went to see him and asked him what was wrong that he wasn't going out. 'Is it your pride that's keeping you? Come on, come on out to church. We'll need to put up with the turf!' Chisholm wouldn't come from his own point: 'It's as well to get the wall up with the turf seeing we haven't got the stones!' Yes, he was like that. Oh, yes. He used to have many people against him (AUTHOR:—which is perhaps not difficult to understand).

I'll tell you something else about him. He was at one time at a Communion. And when it came to the Sunday Communion service, he said when he stood that somebody else would have to take the service, that he wasn't going to: there was something wrong with one that was going forward that day. Oh, he was a very godly man. Anyway, they kept a mark on every one that went to the Communion table to see if anything was wrong about any of them. And there was a widow there that had lost her husband years before that . . . and she was pregnant. He didn't know anything about it, but he said, 'I can't go on— I'm not to go on with the service. You can go on with it if you like, but there's something wrong.' They kept the name of everyone who went forward, to see if he was right: was the minister right, or not?—just to get a claw on Chisholm (who was very unpopular with many). But Chisholm was right . . . yes. When Chisholm looked at you, you felt he could see right through you.

★ ★ ★

I am aware that this is not like a normal biographical sketch and that much of the English may sound quaint to southern ears. I have felt it wise, however, to retain much of Mary's own phraseology. To those who know the Hebrides it will bring memories of the musical speech of warm and kindly people. Their usage of English has in it a beautifully soft and gentle quality. Their spirits are gentle.

May God bless all my readers.

Notes

1 I remember hearing one very sad story. A man, speaking of his spiritual condition, said: 'I went too far in opposing God in revival. I spoke against the moving and from that time God has never spoken to me. I am lost and there is nothing anybody can do for me.' It is many years since I heard of this and have given the sense of what he said as accurately as I can.

2 Pauline Anderson and a friend.

3 It is not discourteous to use surnames in this way in the Highlands, as it might seem in the south.

APPENDIX I

The Place of Reason

Extract from *An Outline of Psychology* by William McDougall.[1]

> The instincts are the prime movers of all human activity; by the conative or impulsive force of some instinct, every train of thought, however cold and passionless it may seem, is borne along towards its end . . . all the complex intellectual apparatus of the most highly developed mind is but the instrument by which these impulses seek their satisfaction . . . Take away these instinctive dispositions, with their powerful mechanisms, and the organism would become incapable of activity of any kind; it would be inert and motionless, like a wonderful piece of clockwork whose mainspring had been removed.

Extract from *Guide to Modern Thought* by C. E. M. Joad.[2]

> [Men] today are fundamentally sceptical of the part played by reasoning in determining our conduct and forming our beliefs. Reason, it is widely suggested, is a mere tool or handmaid of desire. Its function is to secure the ends which we unconsciously set ourselves, by inventing excuses for what we instinctively want to do, and arguments for what we instinctively want to believe . . . .

Psycho-analysts hold, as we have seen, that the forces that dominate our natures are fundamentally instinctive and, therefore, non-rational in character. The unconscious is pictured as a restless sea of instinct and impulse, a sea agitated by gusts of libido, swept by waves of desire, threaded by the currents of urge and drive; and upon these waves and currents, consciousness, with all that it contains, bobs helplessly like a cork. Consciousness is represented, in fact, as a sort of by-product of the unconscious. This general conception is exemplified by the attitude current in psycho-analytic literature to reason.

. . . Of these natural forces we know very little, especially since we have succeeded in evolving reason, one of whose main functions is to rationalise them, and so disguise from us their real character. But reason is itself an expression of these instinctive *natural* forces, one of the latest and the weakest. It is a feeble shoot springing from a deep, dim foundation of unconscious strivings, and maintaining a precarious existence as their apologist and their handmaid.

Reason, in fact, is a mere tool of instinct; it is instinct which determines the occasions of its operation and its function is limited to discovering means for satisfying the instincts which employ it. Professor McDougall's theory of instinct points to the same conclusion. 'The instincts,' it will be remembered, are, on this view, 'the prime movers of all human activity . . . all the complex intellectual apparatus of the most highly developed mind is but the instrument by which these impulses seek their satisfaction.' Reason, in other words, is a mechanism; it is the engine of the personality, and instinct is the steam that sets it going. And, since reason can operate only when driven by the impulsive force of instinct, it can proceed only along the path which instinct indicates to the goal which instinct dictates.[3]

Extract from *Christ in Congo Forests* by Norman P. Grubb.[4]

They are fools who belittle such holy experiences and warn against 'excessive emotionalism'. Such do not even understand the make up of 'Mansoul', still less the ways of the Eternal Lover with His beloved. With sure sense of direction does the inspired Word always point us to the heart, not the mind, as the citadel of Man. It is there that the emotions lie deep-seated, the desires that drive the will, those mysterious fires which burn with the lurid passions of hell, or light up the life with the holy love of heaven, according to the spirit that dwells in them. The mere mind of man, his views and ideas, his intellectual conceits and opinions, are but straw before the whirlwind in the grip of the real inner man of the heart, when it holds the helm. And revivals reach that inner man, and carry the mind along later as captive in its train. They move the deep springs of being, and all else follows: and they do it in earthquake fashion.

Extract from *The Law of Faith* by Norman P. Grubb.[5]

This experience is pre-eminently a manifestation of the Spirit through the emotions. It is a presenting of the personality to God with such a complete abandonment and at such a pitch of intensity that the reason is finally transcended, the conscious being submerged, the love of God and the power of the Spirit flooding in through the whole range of the emotions.

In this rational age, however, we are quick—and foolish— to despise and deride emotion. Such an experience as the above appears either ridiculous, unnecessary or excessive. Not so, indeed. For one thing, it was the experience of Pentecost repeated on the historic occasion when the Gospel was first preached to the Gentiles (Acts 10:44–48): it was common in the early Church (1 Corinthians 14). Paul the rational, the master of logic, thanked God that he spoke with tongues more than they all! For another, the stirring of the emotions is the source of every human activity. No emotion as a driving force, no creative thought; no emotion, no great achievement; no emotion, no deeds of love nor exploits of faith. Love is largely compounded of emotion. God is love.

Therefore in stressing the Baptism of the Holy Ghost with this sign following, the advocates of this teaching are penetrating to the most sensitive, most powerful cord in human nature and are stirring their hearers to seek and find the living God through that avenue. The result is a people whose joy knows no bounds; fervent in testimony, free in prayer, large in heart, wide in generosity, with the warmth in their message and fellowship which attracts more hearers to their usually humble halls than probably any other denomination of equal size.

Notes

[1] Culled from C. E. M. Joad, *Guide to Modern Thought* (Faber & Faber Limited, rev. ed., 1948), p.213.

[2] Joad on contemporary psychoanalysts, *ibid.*, pp.219–21.

[3] It might be fair to add that reason if functioning ideally may very well mirror a reality beyond itself and principles governing it may also have a universal validity. My own quarrel is not with reason as the handmaid of the soul but with the worship of what is sometimes called reason—but which, in fact, is really a distorted reflection of the true.

[4] Norman P. Grubb, *Christ in Congo Forests* (Lutterworth Press, 1945), pp.197–98.

[5] Norman P. Grubb, *The Law of Faith* (Lutterworth Press, 1947), p.88.

APPENDIX II

Tongues as Gift and Tongues as Sign

A full discussion of the Baptism in the Holy Spirit cannot be entered into at this point, but an examination of whether tongues are an indispensable evidence of it may be briefly attempted. The question resolves itself into this: Can an individual be baptized in the Spirit without speaking in tongues? Those who claim tongues as the 'initial evidence' say, 'No.' Many who sympathise with their point of view feel, however, that Scripture does not quite warrant such a dogmatic assertion. Others point to the godly lives and powerful ministries of many who have never spoken in tongues and strongly deny the assertion.

What saith the Scripture? Let it be frankly stated at the outset that in no instance does Scripture state in so many words that tongues must accompany the Baptism. In view of this, how then does the first school conduct its argument? Adherents of this school claim that the Baptism in the Spirit, predicted by John the Baptist and promised by Christ, is incomplete in the case of any individual unless that individual speaks in tongues. They argue that, on the day of Pentecost, the company in the Upper Room were all filled with the Holy Spirit, and all spoke in tongues. The symbol that abode upon each was a cloven tongue.

Further, in three of the five cases in Scripture in which it is recorded that the experience took place it is also recorded that those concerned spoke in tongues. In a fourth case—that of Paul—we are not told what happened at the time of his Baptism but we read later that he spoke in tongues more than all the Corinthians. In the last case, that of the Samaritans, it is obvious from the text that there was an outward evidence of the inner experience—since Simon Magus 'saw that through the laying on of hands the Spirit was given' and desired a like ability to lay on hands. Thus in three cases tongues are mentioned as accompanying the Baptism and in the other two they probably did. Further, in Acts 10:44–47 it is clear that tongues were the accepted evidence of the Baptism. In that instance, the Holy Spirit fell on Cornelius and his company and Peter's friends were amazed that 'on the Gentiles also was poured out the gift of the Holy Ghost. For they heard them speak with tongues, and magnify God.' How did they know that the Holy Ghost had been poured upon them? Simply because they heard them speak with tongues.[1] This is the significance of the word 'for.' These events, this school claims, provide the pattern for all future time.

Is the argument conclusive? Many who believe in tongues and speak in them themselves say, 'No.' 'Even if,' they contend, 'it has been demonstrated that in most cases in Scripture tongues did accompany the Baptism and even if there is no case from which it can be proved that Baptism definitely took place unaccompanied by tongues, it still cannot be categorically stated that tongues are essential to the experience. Scripture just does not say so.' They argue, further, that Paul in 1 Corinthians 12 asks the question, 'Do all speak in tongues?'

This seems weighty. From the context Paul obviously expected the answer, 'No!' and with such an answer he was obviously content. Now Paul would never have been content that a believer should have continued without the

Baptism in the Spirit, as is clear from the case of the Ephesian twelve in Acts 19. Are these people then, to whom he refers in 1 Corinthians 12, Spirit-baptized believers who do not speak in tongues, and if so is the argument against the necessity of tongues conclusive?

The first school denies it. Paul, so the argument goes, is here speaking of the possession of the gift of tongues, which is quite a different thing from the sign of tongues witnessed at the Baptism. The people he addresses here would speak in tongues once—at the time of their Baptism—but, not receiving the gift, would not give utterances bearing interpretation. In short, distinction is made between tongues as a gift and tongues as a sign, which distinction, it is argued, may be often seen in present-day cases.[2]

There is a second group of opponents who go much further. Quoting 1 Corinthians 12:13 ('For in one Spirit were we all baptized into one body, whether Jews or Greeks, whether bond or free; and were all made to drink of one Spirit'), they maintain that all Christians receive the Baptism in the Spirit at conversion (i.e. they come into the Body of Christ) and that, of course, there is no thought of speaking in tongues when this happens.

This spreads the argument further than the immediate purpose of this appendix and a full discussion follows in Appendix 3 below.

To give a fair and unbiased summing-up is not easy. Had the writer been asked to do so in his earlier Pentecostal experience, he would unhesitatingly have maintained that those who insisted upon tongues as the initial evidence had run quite beyond Scripture and that from the text it would appear that Baptism might well take place without this accompanying phenomenon.

The years have brought a change and significances hidden in Acts 2 have emerged which were not at first apparent.

Notice the tremendous prominence given to the tongue in this chapter. The Holy Spirit seems to have been symbolised by wind ('there came from heaven a sound as of the rushing of a mighty wind') and by fire ('And there appeared unto them tongues parting asunder, like as of fire, and it sat upon each one of them'). Why a tongue? Why not a head to symbolise intellect? (Though from the conduct and attitude of so much of the Western Church, one might almost imagine it had been so.) Why not shoulders to bear burden, or hands to work, or feet to run with the gospel, or even a heart to love? Why a tongue? Let it be said pointedly: the Baptism is not referred to as a baptism of love, but as a baptism of Power and as nothing else: 'Tarry . . . in [Jerusalem] until ye be clothed with power from on high'—'Ye shall receive power, when the Holy Ghost is come upon you: and ye shall be my witnesses both in Jerusalem, and in all Judaea and Samaria, and unto the uttermost part of the earth.' 'Power!' 'Witnesses!' The key lies here. Those baptized were to carry the gospel. Without the Baptism they were not equipped to fulfil their mission. The power was to enable them to witness. How were they to witness? With the tongue! By preaching! 'Go ye into all the world, and preach the gospel.' Hence the symbol of the cloven tongue! Hence the fact that their every tongue was affected and set on fire! 'They all began to speak in tongues as the Spirit gave them utterance' (Acts 2:4).

Now what is the immediate effect upon an individual of first speaking in tongues? It causes a loosening of the organ and a practical ability to allow it to be controlled by the felt power of the Holy Spirit. Not only is the human spirit energised under the unction but the actual organ of speech comes under direct control, although the human control is not thereby destroyed. It is as though a guiding hand is superimposed upon a pilot's hand as he steers his craft. He can break the control. So the person speaking in tongues

under God's control may break that control, although he
never should do so. Now it is much easier to allow God to
control one's tongue in a language which the intellect does
not understand, than it is to do so in one's own language
when the understood words are apt to distract the mind
and break the concentration. By learning the spiritual
lesson through tongues, one is deepened and prepared for
the reception of the more important gifts of prophecy and
interpretation and of inspired preaching.

In view of the tremendous emphasis upon the tongue in
this vital chapter it would seem very dangerous to preach
that the Baptism in the Spirit may be complete without the
tongue being affected. Anointings and unctionings there
may be, but is there not a part of the personality left
undeveloped if the tongue remains unaffected? Let an
unbaptized Christian compare himself not with his Pentecostal brethren but with what he himself might be, or
become, with the Baptism. No doubt Apollos, prior to his
probable Baptism, was in many ways a greater man than
some of the humble Spirit-baptized believers of his day.
But was he a greater man than he would become after such
a Baptism? Too often we hear of prominent men, such as
Finney and Spurgeon, who are not definitely known to
have spoken in tongues (although in Finney's case the
evidence suggests that he did), being compared with some
poor humble Pentecostal believer who does speak in
tongues. Compare Spurgeon with what he might have
been or, if comparison with others is insisted upon, then
compare with Paul who exercised an apostolic ministry, or
with people in our own day who are manifesting a ministry
more exactly on the lines and in the power of the early
apostles.[3]

Finally, if tongues are not sufficiently emphasised there
is a grave danger of seekers being cheated of their full
inheritance through mistakenly accepting an incomplete
experience as the full Baptism. In my own case I was

deeply moved by the Spirit and convinced that I had been baptized some hours before I first spoke in tongues and it is significant that when the latter occurred it seemed as though the baptizing Power had found the desired channel of expression. There was a feeling of completion with tongues utterance.[4]

Some believe that the Baptism may be obtained by faith and undoubtedly many have obtained deep experience in the Spirit along this line. But there are grave dangers. Salvation comes through faith—but is not itself believing. It is a real experience which takes place as a result of believing. So with the Baptism. The seeker does not receive it merely by believing that he has it. Many have tried this and found that in fact nothing has happened. There is a difference between claiming something by faith and actually receiving it. A person should claim but he should also tarry until that which is claimed is received. Too many have been tricked by substituting the believing for the receiving and gone empty away. Long ago Finney pointed out this fallacy in connection with 'the prayer of faith'—showing the danger of a belief that rested upon nothing but itself. An example will simplify the matter. A missionary is engaged in God's work and is in need of a hundred pounds. He takes this by faith and in due time God honours this faith and sends the money enabling him to meet his commitments. Now until the hundred pounds is received, he remains unable to meet those commitments. His belief pays no bills. There is a difference between believing that the money will come—nay, that in God's purposes it is already as good as his—and his actual, practical receiving of it. So with the Baptism. Let it be taken by faith, but do not let the person so doing depart from the condition of tarrying until he receives in practice. It is obvious that in Acts 2 something other than an inner faith-experience took place. Those seeking had faith assuredly—they tarried—but the actual reception of the

Spirit was a matter, not of faith, but of knowledge and experience.

Notes

1 There may be other evidences of the Baptism, but it is interesting that this is the only evidence that Scripture itself cites.

2 There is also a third school which feels that at initial Baptism persons are enabled to speak in tongues and are thereafter able so to do, without having received the gift of tongues. Such people, they maintain, may speak in tongues, as for example in private prayer, but will be unable to give utterances bearing interpretation unless they receive the distinct gift of tongues. People who hold this view distinguish between speaking in tongues at the Baptism and exercising the gift. This view should have some consideration, since many people do have a distinct experience of receiving the ability to give utterances bearing interpretation, long after they have first been baptized and spoken in tongues.

3 After this book was written but before publication I came on the writing of Donald Lee Barnett and Jeffrey P. McGregor in their work *Speaking in Other Tongues* (Seattle: Community Chapel Publications, 1986), and am persuaded by the evidence they produce that all three men were baptized in the Spirit and all spoke in tongues. This matter is of such importance that it is given fuller treatment in Appendix 7 below.

4 One problem which has often mystified the writer concerns many of our brethren who claim to be fully baptized in the Spirit, but do not speak in tongues. Some of those do not altogether oppose or deny tongues. Yet they do not themselves speak in them, nor do their companies. Often, too, they criticise our strong emphasis upon them. The question arises: 'Why do at least some of their members not sometimes speak in this way, if their experience is fully on the lines of the New Testament?' It may be all very well to say that Scripture does not actually say that all must speak in tongues. But surely some should. When none do, a re-thinking of the position is surely indicated.

APPENDIX III

Further Notes on the Baptism in the Spirit

Many critics of Pentecostal doctrine hold that at conversion believers immediately receive the Holy Spirit and that there is no further baptism promised them. They concede that there was a distinct experience on the day of Pentecost, accompanied by tongues, but that, they say, ushered in a new order. They also concede that for a number of years at the beginning of the dispensation Pentecostal phenomena continued but maintain that as soon as the new order was established, the required miraculous attestation of God to its authority was withdrawn.[1] With the close of the canon of Scripture, they say, there was no longer need for tongues, prophecy and the other miraculous gifts. In the early days the Church did not have the Scriptures which we have. With their completion, the need for miraculous manifestations ceased. Men are now walking entirely by faith with the Scriptures as their sole guide. Where once there was the need for prophecy, for example, this need is amply met by the completed Scriptures.

This is peculiarly misguided reasoning. To begin with, there is no evidence to support it. Indeed the evidence is all on the other side. Miraculous phenomena continued long after the close of the canon of Scripture. There are frequent references to this in the early Fathers. In the second century, Irenaeus wrote:

> Even among the brethren frequently in a case of necessity, when a whole Church united in much fasting and prayer, the Spirit has returned to the ex-animated body, and the man was granted to the prayers of the saints.
>
> . . . Some, indeed, most certainly and truly cast out demons. So that frequently those persons themselves that were cleaned from wicked spirits, believed and were received into the Church. Others have the knowledge of things to come, as also visions and prophetic communications: others heal the sick by the imposition of hands, and restore them to health. And moreover, as we said above, even the dead have been raised, and continued with us many years. And why should we say more? It is impossible to tell the number of the gifts the Church throughout the world received from God, and the deeds performed in the name of Jesus Christ.
>
> . . . As we hear many of the brethren in the Church who have prophetic gifts, and who speak in all tongues through the Spirit, and who also bring to light the secret things of men for their benefit, and who expound the mysteries of God . . . .[2]

Augustine also testifies to similar phenomena[3] and there is an abundance of evidence for this in the present day.

Secondly, it will not do to search in the Bible for the last recorded instance of an individual speaking in tongues or prophesying and solemnly pronounce: 'This is the last time we read of this kind of occurrence and so we may conclude that it ceased from then onwards.'

After all, there must inevitably be a last recorded instance. Since history clearly shows that such phenomena continued, the case falls to the ground. Such diminution as occurred indicates a setting-in of spiritual coldness, rather than an advance to maturity.

It was in fact with the coming of coldness and death, during later ages, that the miraculous greatly declined. As Wesley said:

It does not appear, that these extraordinary gifts of the Holy Ghost were common in the Church for more than two or three centuries. We seldom hear of them after that fatal period, when the Emperor Constantine called himself a Christian; and from a vain imagination of promoting the Christian cause thereby, heaped riches, and power, and honour, upon the Christians in general; but in particular, upon the Christian Clergy. From this time they almost totally ceased: very few instances of the kind were found. The cause of this was not (as has been vulgarly supposed), 'because there was no more occasion for them', because all the world was become Christians. This is a miserable mistake: not a twentieth part of it was then nominally Christians. The real cause was, 'the love of many,' almost of all Christians, so called, was 'waxed cold.' The Christians had no more of the Spirit of Christ, than the other Heathens. The Son of Man, when He came to examine his Church, could hardly 'find faith upon earth.' This was the real cause, why the extraordinary gifts of the Holy Ghost were no longer to be found in the Christian Church; because the Christians were turned Heathens again, and had only a dead form left.[4]

As has been indicated, it is as reasonable to say that salvation has ceased since the canon of Scripture is closed, as it is to say that the Baptism in the Spirit is not for our day. Salvation meets man's personal age-abiding need; the Baptism empowers him to meet the age-abiding need of others. As the continuance of the one is essential, so is the continuance of the other.

This school places great emphasis on 1 Corinthians 12:13 and Romans 8:9 in support of its viewpoint. This, to begin with, is strange, since these Scriptures refer to those who were undoubtedly the subjects of Pentecostal experience. To apply such verses to what may be termed the 'later order' of things seems unreasonable and indeed can scarcely be countenanced.

The verses read:

> For in one Spirit were we all baptized into one body, whether Jews or Greeks, whether bond or free; and were all made to drink of one Spirit (1 Cor 12:13).

> If any man have not the Spirit of Christ, he is none of His (Rom 8:9).

It is argued that immediately a man becomes a Christian he enters the Body of Christ which is the Church. His entrance to this is by Baptism in the Spirit—and this is the only baptism which there is in the Spirit.

What actually do the verses mean? The first reference has presented much difficulty through the use of the words 'in' and 'into.' Let us first consider baptism generally:

    (a) Christians are baptized in water into the name of the Father and the Son and the Holy Spirit;

    (b) The Israelites were baptized in the cloud and in the sea unto Moses;

    (c) John baptized in water unto repentance.

Now men are not baptized in water to make them followers of Christ, but because they already are His followers. The Israelites were not baptized in the cloud and in the sea to make them followers of Moses. They were so baptized because they were his followers. Men were not baptized by John to make them repent but because they had repented.

In the same way, men are not baptized in the Spirit to make them members of the Church, the Body of Christ, but because they are members of that Church. Thus Baptism in the Spirit is not the initiation into the Body, but is a distinct and different experience from it. Conversion gives entrance there—and on the grounds of membership of the living Church, Baptism in the Holy Spirit is given. Hence the words: 'For to you is the promise [of the outpoured Spirit], and to your children, and to all that are afar off, even as many as the Lord our God shall call unto him' (Acts 2:39).

Thus the Baptism in the Spirit cannot be equated with conversion or initiation into the Body of Christ. John the Baptist said: 'He shall baptize you with the Holy Ghost and with fire' (Mt 3:11).

This is obviously different from the baptism to which Paul refers when he says: 'In one Spirit' or, as the Authorised Version reads, 'By one Spirit were ye all baptized into one Body.' In the first case the baptism is into the Spirit, and Christ is the Baptizer. In the second the baptism is into the Body and the Spirit is the Baptizer.[5]

We come now to the second text, '. . . if any man have not the Spirit of Christ, he is none of his.' From this the dispensationalists argue that all who are His must have the Spirit. The argument depends on two assumptions: (1) that the Spirit of Christ is synonymous with the Holy Spirit, and (2) that 'to have the Spirit' is 'to have been baptized in the Spirit.' If both of these assumptions are granted, then the verse must be interpreted to mean that all Christians are *ipso facto* baptized in the Spirit. This clearly contradicts the Pentecostals' position, according to which conversion is a prerequisite for the Baptism but does not in itself include the Baptism.

Three lines of defence are open.

1. We might distinguish between the expressions 'Spirit of God' (the Holy Spirit) and 'Spirit of Christ.' This, however, seems to me to introduce a duality quite foreign to the general New Testament teaching. Indeed Acts 16:6–7 seems to show the expressions used synonymously.

2. The word S/spirit as used here may carry the thought of attitude or disposition as, for example, 'Let this mind be in you which was also in Christ Jesus.' We speak of a Christlike spirit—'spirit' not here referring to the Third Person of the Trinity. Christ's spirit was meek, loving, forbearing; and it may be said that men are to have the same spirit. Thus the word could be used here in a general

sense with no reference to the Holy Spirit. I do not myself take this view.

3. Speaking of the Holy Spirit to His disciples, 'He,' said Christ, 'is with you, and he shall be in you.' It may be argued that the Spirit's presence 'with' rather than 'in' is indicated in the verse '. . . if any man hath not the Spirit of Christ, he is none of his.' Even had the word 'in' been used, as it is elsewhere, there could still be a distinction between 'in' in a general sense and 'in' as 'possessing.' Now the latter is the baptizing sense and is obviously not relevant to the verse under discussion—since many belonged to Christ long before they received this experience, as, for example, the Ephesian twelve.

Similarly the phenomena of Cornelius's case are explained. Here the door is being thrown open to the Gentiles. It is necessary for Peter to have some outward evidence of what is happening to the Gentiles. Again the phenomena are viewed as marking a new beginning.

This might sound feasible but unfortunately for this school these are not the only recorded cases of Baptism in the Spirit. The case of the Ephesian twelve of Acts 19, already cited, does not fall into this category. These men were not pioneers in any sense. Their case was the beginning of nothing in particular. They met Paul about nineteen years after Pentecost. They had not been baptized in the Spirit and Paul questioned them about it. Whether they were Christians or not when Paul met them is not significant. They certainly were before he baptized them in water. And upon these baptized converts he laid his hands and they were filled with the Spirit and spoke in tongues and prophesied. Again let it be asked: In what way does their experience, prior to the coming of Paul's hands upon them, differ from that of tens of thousands of Christians today, who have been baptized in water, but have never had such a filling of the Spirit? Paul was not content to leave them without the second experience and the questions arise: Can we prove any real difference in our case and, if not, should we be content to remain in such a condition?

Notes

[1] Was Pentecost merely a 'beginning'?

Those who take this view explain the laying of hands on the Samaritans as follows: For long there had been a rift between Samaritan and Jew. This was not to be reflected in the Christian Church. Had the Samaritans received the Holy Spirit independently, such might have continued; but to emphasise their dependence upon and identification with Jerusalem, it is suggested that the Holy Spirit was withheld from them until Peter and John went down from Jerusalem and laid hands on them. Thus the time lapse (for time lapse there certainly was) between their conversion and Baptism in the Spirit is explained. It was a beginning for the Samaritans. Presumably later Samaritan converts are viewed as having received the Spirit immediately on conversion without accompanying phenomena.

[2] Translations from Eusebius' *Ecclesiastical History* are culled from George Jeffreys, *Pentecostal Rays* (Elim Publishing Co., 1933), p.195. Eusebius's source is Irenaeus, *Against Heresies*, ii. 31, 32 and v. 6.

[3] *The City of God, xxii.* 8, presents a detailed account of miracles of healing and exorcism known to Augustine personally. The last of these concludes on a note that makes most Pentecostal meetings nowadays seem sedate by comparison. When the miracle became apparent to the gathered company of Christians, 'they exulted in God's praise with wordless voice, and so great was the sound that our ears could hardly bear it.' My thanks go to Dr. Marsha Daigle and Dr. Pamela Jackson for pointing me to this and other references in Augustine's writings.

[4] John Wesley, 'The More Excellent Way,' Sermon 94 in *Sermons on Several Occasions*, 2 vols (J. Kershaw, 1825), vol. 2, pp.431–32.

[5] A study of the Greek prepositions *en* (by, in) and *eis* (into) is very helpful in clarifying this whole subject.

APPENDIX IV

The 'Set' Prophet and Directional Prophecy

In some circles the practice has developed of having 'set' prophets, who hold a distinct office and are themselves distinct from ordinary members of the congregation who have the gift of prophecy. These are recognised and in many instances, I understand, regulate governmental matters within the church, ostensibly by virtue of their special gift and calling. Thus prophecy becomes directional and governmental. The question arises, 'Is it Scriptural?'

Those who argue in favour of the practice make much of the case of Agabus, who indicated what awaited Paul in Jerusalem on a particular occasion, and the case of Timothy, who was told to stir up the gift that was in him which was given him by prophecy through the laying on of the hands of the presbytery.

It seems to me that those cases prove little. The first states a matter of fact and contains no general direction. The second relates to the giving of a spiritual gift and indicates a spiritual ministry.

Now there is a danger in swinging to either extreme on this question. It must be allowed that God can give direction in prophecy. That He gives general spiritual direction through it is admitted on all sides; that an individual may be the subject of it is proved; that it may contain personal direction is reasonable and has in fact in many cases happened—but this having been said, it must be added that there is a grave danger of making an exceptional occurrence a standard for general practice. There is always a danger in attempting to institutionalise religion. It is too easy to fall into the practice of looking for a word of prophecy and for the prophet to feel that he is expected to give it, and of something other than a genuine utterance resulting. Was there such an institution in Paul's day?— almost certainly not! Neither is there any suggestion of the Old Testament system of 'enquiring of the Lord' being carried into the New in association with prophecy.

By all means let a genuine prophet, if given a revelation from the Lord for a company or an individual, be free to give it. But let it be discerned. Let the person receiving it take it before God and accept or reject it before Him. Let others judge. Let it by no means be received merely because it purports to be prophecy. God will have no false priesthood between the soul and Himself—and this is apt to happen if too unheeding obedience is given to the voice of prophecy. On the other hand, let a person beware of how he deals with genuine prophecy. If there is a witness to the word within, he will disregard it to his cost. The dangers lie at the extremes. The spiritual mind has little difficulty in distinguishing the genuine from the man-made; and the gift properly used to public and personal edification results in extremely deep spiritual blessing.

In matters of church government, prophecy can be useful in providing illumination and guidance, but the New Testament does not indicate that prophecy should be used as a general instrument of government.

APPENDIX V

The Passivity of Pentecost

The passivity of Pentecost is not the passivity of death, nor is it the dangerous passivity which leaves the soul open to every wind that blows. It is a controlled state, but one in which the carnal and natural human processes tainted by the Fall are reckoned as dead—'crucified with Christ.' The personality is, instead, opened to God in order that divine life and divine processes may replace natural life and activity; that, in short, the life of Christ may literally be made manifest.

There is a practical psychological way in which the doctrine of crucifixion of the self-life, so strongly emphasised by Paul in his epistle to the Romans, actually works. The 'passivity' is an active passivity. It is as though one goes down into death and rises again to newness of life. The same natural parts and faculties of personality are used, but they are first renewed and transformed. Their control and direction is altogether different. Where previously they were turned by self to self for self, they are now directed by God to God for God. The egocentric has become the God-centred. Instead of man controlling himself, God now controls man. The control, however, is voluntarily yielded. As Paul might say: The old man, the fallen Adam-man, is crucified and the new man, the Christ-man, is alive and active. The activity springs from deep spiritual founts. It is produced by the activity of the Holy Spirit in an individual whose will has accepted the passive state and whose personality is thereby closed to the fallen natural processes and activity.

This is an introduction to the laws of the eternal, and all life may well be of this glorious nature in Heaven. God will be all in all and His creatures perfect and in harmony with Himself and with His laws. Such states, instead of producing abject and servile slavery, frustration and misery, gave unspeakable liberty and joy. Free will once became self will, and produced hell on earth. Divinely controlled it will produce Heaven.

Finally, the question: In such a state, is the activity divine or human? The mainspring is divine, but it gathers the human in its flow and produces that which bears the marks of the personality of the individual—but the divine stamp is upon all. Man, as many realise, is not himself a fundamental self-sufficient being. He has no control of his birth, or of his death, or of many of his states. His roots lie elsewhere than in himself and he seeks satisfaction elsewhere than in himself. Deeply analysed, these roots prove to be in God, or in the devil; and for an individual to accept the passivity outlined here is not so much to yield a will which is totally free, as to yield the illusion of this, and in reality to transfer his allegiance from the devil and his works to God. The fact that man is not completely free and therefore, in a sense, not free at all, is of vital importance. The illusion that he is, is responsible for a great deal of opposition to the demand of God—which openly claims complete obedience. Men too often mistakenly think they are being asked to surrender independence which they feel is an inalienable human right, for bondage which they feel is beneath the dignity of man. This is just not so. When men are asked to allow God to control them they are merely being asked to transfer their allegiance. Already, indeed from birth, they are conditioned and quite dependent creatures. They are born disposed and conditioned towards evil, and are generally blind to that fact and its corollaries—one of which is the illusion of free will.

Thus men are in bondage to their passions and their passions were let loose upon them by an act of self-will. Man grasped the reins and has steadily driven on to destruction. The bondservice of Satan was mistaken for independence and the real independence, once so richly enjoyed in subjection to God, has been lost. Pentecost gives the first-fruits of redemption and restoration. Perhaps man's fundamental error has been: '*My* right to *myself* . . . Not God's will—but *my* will be done.' Pentecost declares and practises: '*God's* right to me.'—and that, not merely theoretically as an act of belief, but practically, and in the physical body. This becomes very manifest when one is under Divine unction and control for use in the gifts of the Spirit.

It should be emphasised that in this passive state, man does not become a mere automaton. God does not control a dead man. He guides and empowers a man who is alive to Himself but dead to the fallen part of his human nature. God works through him, not independently of him. Thereby his personality is not destroyed but empowered. To allow such to happen is not to commit suicide but to enter fuller life. It is a matter of exchanging a wrong control for a right, for, as has been indicated, man is inevitably controlled by something, or someone. It is not to have faculties destroyed—but to have them turned in a right direction and functioning in a right way.

APPENDIX VI

Joel's Prediction

Joel predicted an outpouring of the Spirit upon all flesh in the 'last days.' With the outpouring he associated astronomic and earthly phenomena. This, he said, was immediately to precede the day of the Lord. The verses read:

> 'And it shall come to pass afterward, that I will pour out my spirit upon all flesh; and your sons and your daughters shall prophesy, your old men shall dream dreams, your young men shall see visions: and also upon the servants and upon the handmaids in those days will I pour out my spirit. And I will shew wonders in the heavens and in the earth, blood, and fire, and pillars of smoke. The sun shall be turned into darkness, and the moon into blood, before the great and terrible day of the Lord come (Joel 2:28–31).

This poses certain problems and raises most interesting speculations.

Obviously the prophecy was not fully fulfilled on the day of Pentecost with which Peter first associates it. An outpouring of the Spirit certainly took place then, but the astronomic signs which were linked with it were not fulfilled, nor did the age end. Many feel that the 'last times' is in fact a long period stretching from the day of

Pentecost to the close of the dispensation. The 'former rain' fell at the beginning of the era, and at the end the deluge of the former and latter rain coming together is to be expected. This did not occur on the day of Pentecost, nor has it yet occurred. So in all probability there will yet be a world-wide awakening, of which many feel there are already indications. Towards the end, spiritual activity will undoubtedly increase—both good and evil. While there will probably be more Christians alive than in any other age, the mass of the people will be unbelieving. Hence it will still be true that in general the 'Son of Man when he cometh will not find faith on the earth.' Wickedness will, no doubt, reach new depths. In my view, there will be an increasing polarisation of both good and evil as Christ's return approaches.

In Matthew 24:29–30 Christ said:

> But immediately, after the tribulation of those days, the sun shall be darkened, and the moon shall not give her light, and the stars shall fall from heaven, and the powers of heaven shall be shaken: and then shall appear the sign of the Son of man in heaven: and then shall all the tribes of the earth mourn, and they shall see the Son of man coming on the clouds of heaven with power and great glory.

These Scriptures seem to refer to the same events. The tribulation, in my view, is a long period stretching from the destruction of Jerusalem, A.D.70 (when it undoubtedly began[1]) to the time of Christ's return. Again strange astronomic phenomena are predicted.

There is reason to believe, from these and many other prophecies, that Christ's return is imminent. The signs are almost all fulfilled and while the subject of the Second Coming cannot be fully explored in this context, we can say that Scripture gives us grounds for expecting an increasing outpouring of the Spirit, accompanied by spiritual gifts and world-wide revival as the end draws near.

The Pentecostal and Charismatic movements may be the first streams of the great flood.

Notes

[1] On going out of the temple for the last time, Christ's attention was drawn to the stones of the building and He indicated that there would not be one left upon another that would not be thrown down. His disciples questioned Him as to when these things would be, and what would be the sign of His Coming and of the end of the world. In His reply He associates the destruction of Jerusalem and the temple with the great tribulation. Thus the beginning of the tribulation period is pinpointed. Men rejected the Prince of Peace, and from AD 70 to the present time almost two-thirds of the period has been occupied by war. I regard the tribulation as a lengthy period stretching from AD 70 to the coming of Christ, with trouble possibly intensifying towards the end. I do not associate the tribulation with Daniel's 'seventieth week' as do the Futurist school of prophecy. I agree with the Historicist view that Daniel's seventieth week followed his sixty-ninth week immediately and is now past history. To insert an unspecified period of time between week 69 and week 70 is to make a nonsense of our normal use of time as a measurement.

APPENDIX VII

Evidence that Finney, Moody and Spurgeon Spoke in Tongues

Donald Lee Barnett and Jeffrey P. McGregor maintain in their *Speaking in Other Tongues: A Scholarly Defense* that Finney, Moody and Spurgeon all spoke in tongues.[1] They write:

> Here is what [Finney] wrote about his mighty post-salvation experience that equipped him to wrestle the devil for the prize of perhaps half a million souls:
>
> > . . . I received a mighty baptism in the Holy Ghost . . . . No words can express the wonderful love that was shed abroad in my heart. I wept aloud with joy and love; and I do not know but I should say, *I literally bellowed out the unutterable gushings of my heart.*
>
> . . . As the evangelist [Finney] explains in his autobiography, he made a few attempts to tell people about some of his remarkable experiences in prayer, but was greeted with such surprise and skepticism that he soon learned to keep quiet about them . . . . Sedley D. Kinne's book, *Spirituals*, tells of an English woman who heard him pray in an unknown tongue during family devotions. It was said that Finney believed the language was a special gift God had given him. When the

Pentecostal revival came, the woman recognized in it the same manifestation she had seen in Finney.

. . . Dwight L. Moody . . . did not think Pentecost was a miracle that would never recur. In one of his last sermons in Boston, Moody said, 'I believe Pentecost was but a specimen day. I think the church has made this woeful mistake that Pentecost was a miracle that is not to be repeated.' . . . [The] following incident took place during Moody's ministry in England, as recounted by his friend, Robert Boyd:

> On the following Sunday night, when I got to the rooms of the Y.M.C.A. I found the meetings on fire. The young men were speaking in tongues and prophesying. What on earth did it all mean? Only that Moody had been addressing them that afternoon.

. . . [One] evening in Dallas . . . when Moody got up to preach, he addressed the amazed congregation in a strange tongue. With obvious effort he shifted into English and launched into his message without remark. When Brother Poole, of Pasadena, turned in alarm to the person next to him, he was quietly assured: 'It's all right. This is that which was spoken by the prophet Joel!' Poole began to seek the Holy Spirit, and later joined the Pentecostals.

At a meeting in Los Angeles, Dr R. A. Torrey told of a service in London where Moody took the pulpit to preach and instead broke into another language. He tried again, with similar results. The third time, after prayer and praise, he was able to preach his message.

. . . We come now to that prince of preachers, Charles H. Spurgeon. Was it his golden oratory alone that packed the Metropolitan Tabernacle with spiritually hungry Londoners year after year? No, it was the anointing of God and, apparently in spite of himself, Spurgeon manifested the inward power with the outward sign. A British preacher told how the evangelist once asked his audience to forgive him that when he got especially happy in the Lord, 'I break forth into a kind of gibberish which I do not myself understand.'

Note

1 The following extracts are taken from Barnett and McGregor, *Speaking in Other Tongues*, pp.250–52. The sources on which they draw are Finney's *Autobiography*, p.20; Lennard Darbee, *Tongues: The Dynamite of God* (Seattle: Lennard Darbee, n.d.), p.24, which also cites S. D. Kinne's *Spirituals* (no bibliographic data provided); Elmer C. Miller, *Pentecost Examined by a Baptist Lawyer* (Springfield, Mo.: Gospel Publishing House, 1936), p.35; and Robert Boyd, *The Lives and Labours of Moody and Sankey* (Toronto: A. W. Hobey, 1876), p.47. For further information, see Barnett and McGregor, *ibid.*

NOTE TO READERS

If you would like to enquire further about issues raised in this book or if you feel that the author could be of help, you are invited to write to him at 27 Denholm Street, Greenock, PA16 8RH, Scotland, or telephone 0475 87432.

It may also be of interest to know that the author is normally involved in five conferences in Scotland each year—New Year, Easter, July, August and October. Friends gather from many parts of Britain. An open invitation is extended to all and particularly to those interested in the Baptism in the Holy Spirit and related themes. Details will be provided on enquiry.

BY THE SAME AUTHOR

Reflections on the Baptism in the Holy Spirit £2.25 Published in December 1987, this book has already proved very popular and is being used in bringing people into the Baptism in the Spirit. It has been described as one of the clearest, most incisive books on this subject.

Reflections on the Gifts of the Spirit £2.75 Deals in an original way with its subject. The chapters on miracles, healings and discernment (with exorcism) have roused great interest. Anecdotes and illustrations have been much appreciated.

Reflections on a Song of Love £1.25 A highly original commentary on 1 Cor. 13. The drawing power of love pervades this fascinating study. The book is already proving very popular.

A Trumpet Call to Women £2.50 This book has been deeply appreciated. It presents a strong case from Scripture for greater involvement of women in ministry. It throws much light on those portions of the Bible which on the surface seem to put women in a subject role. Contains a very interesting testimony—that of Elizabeth H. Taylor, a lady much used of God. A stirring book, demanding a response—a call to action.

Battle for the Body £2.95 It will take courage to face the truths highlighted in this vitally interesting approach to the fundamental issues of sanctification. The second part presents the powerful testimony of John Hamilton—a preacher widely known and loved.

Consider Him £2.25 Christ Himself seems to speak from the pages of this book, which is enhanced by the testimony of Jennifer Jack, whose selfless presentation truly leaves the reader to consider Christ.

These books are available from various bookshops, but may also be obtained directly from NEW DAWN BOOKS, c/o 27 Denholm Street, Greenock, PA16 8RH (please enclose 30p for postage and packaging).